Legends of
North-East Scotland

Stories for the young and the not so young

by

FENTON WYNESS

Illustrated by the author

Gramercy Publishing Company · New York

FOREWORD

The North-east corner of Scotland is particularly rich in legends and folk-tales. Down the centuries, these have been told and re-told, many of them being familiar to the older generation. With the changing pattern of life, however, the up and coming generations have little opportunity of hearing these tales which are an essential part of the folk-tradition of our countryside.

Most of the stories included in this collection appeared in my *Book of Legends* (1942) and *Second Book of Legends* (1943), but as both these have been out of print for over twenty-five years and as second-hand copies are now difficult to obtain, I readily agreed to the request to re-issue them in a single volume. They now appear under the title *Legends of North-East Scotland* and I hope the book will help to keep alive some of the traditional tales of the area.

45 Salisbury Terrace   FENTON WYNESS
Aberdeen

The Black Colonel

About a mile below the Linn of Dee is the little hamlet of Inverey. It stands at the junction of the Ey with the River Dee, and is one of the most picturesque villages in the county.

At the west end of the hamlet is the castle of Inverey, now a mere heap of rubble, but in the seventeenth century the stronghold of the Farquharsons of Inverey.

The most outstanding member of the family was John, 3rd of Inverey. He was a tall, dark-complexioned man, and a fearless fighter, known to all as 'The Black Colonel'.

The Black Colonel spent most of his time at Inverey Castle, where he lived with a small band of retainers, led by Alisdair McDougal. When the Colonel wished to call his henchman McDougal, he did not ring a bell or shout for him, but fired a pistol at a targe which hung on the wall, so those who formed the Colonel's household had to have strong nerves. Much of the time was passed at Inverey preparing for war, and when Viscount Dundee sent a letter to the Colonel asking him to raise an army he required no second bidding.

I

Alisdair McDougal was sent round the Farquharson lands with the fiery cross—a cross made from two pieces of wood, one end burning and the other dipped in blood – for this was the signal for all the clan to gather. As he ran, he gave the Farquharsons' battle slogan *Carn na cuimhne*. In a very short time the Farquharson men gathered at Inverey Castle and, headed by the Black Colonel, marched off to war.

The Colonel and his men took part in the battle of Killiecrankie, which you will remember was fought in 1689. The Farquharsons lost many men, but the Black Colonel and a number of his retainers escaped, returning to Inverey Castle, where they remained in hiding.

All went well for a time, but one night, after the household had gone to bed, there was a knocking at the courtyard gate. McDougal hastened to see who could be about the glen at that late hour. It was an old woman who had come from Braemar to warn the Colonel that the 'red-coats' – the name given to the Royalist soldiers – were coming up the valley in search of the Killiecrankie fugitives.

The Black Colonel leapt from his bed and, with McDougal at his heels, took the little path up Glen Ey. Nor were they any too soon, for by the time they had reached the cottage of Loinavoick the 'red-coats' were at the castle gate.

There was a sharp encounter between the few retainers left in the castle as a rear-guard, and the 'red-coats', who easily overpowered them and set the building on fire. As the fire spread to the upper storeys a heavily cloaked figure was seen to dash from the burning building, through the smoke and up the glen. The 'red-coats', thinking it was the Black Colonel, gave chase, but it proved to be his housekeeper, Annie Ban, who, by her daring, had allowed the Colonel a little more time to get safely away. After questioning her regarding the whereabouts of the Colonel, of which she pleaded complete ignorance, the 'red-coats' let her go and returned to the castle, which was now well alight.

On the summit of Creag a' Chait, the hill above the castle, the Black Colonel with his henchman watched his homestead burning in the valley below. McDougal felt so sorry for him that he dared not express his sympathy. Suddenly the Colonel broke into loud laughter, explaining that he had put all the gun-powder into the Charter room, which was securely locked so that when the flames reached it there would be a violent explosion and many of the 'red-coats' would be killed. Hardly had he finished speaking when there was a loud bang which resounded among the high hills of Inverey. The flames had reached the gun-powder. How many 'red-coats' were killed nobody will ever know, but

3

'the Black Colonel watched his
homestead burning'

in the morning a small band of them still remained in the hamlet and from there set out in parties to search for the Colonel.

He was never found, for he hid in a cave cut out of the rocks in the Ey valley, and Annie Ban carried food to him and his faithful McDougal every day.

When the 'red-coats' left Inverey he came down from his hiding place and sadly inspected his burnt-out home. Nothing daunted, however, he rallied his men and put the 'red-coats' to flight in a skirmish which took place on the lower slopes of Craig Choinnich at Braemar.

John Farquharson, the Black Colonel, died about the year 1698, and expressed the wish to be buried with his ancestors in the little graveyard at Inverey. His request, however, was forgotten, and he was buried at Castleton of Braemar with all the ceremony due to a chieftain.

The day after he was buried passers-by were horrified to see the Black Colonel's coffin resting on the ground beside his grave, and arrangements were made for it to be buried again. Three times it was buried and three times it was found above ground. Only then did his retainers remember the Colonel's dying request to be buried at Inverey so, as the road to Inverey was blocked with snow, they made a raft and placing their dead chief's coffin on it, pulled it up the River Dee to Inverey. Here they buried the Black Colonel among his ancestors.

The old graveyard at Inverey can still be picked out with difficulty, although now completely overgrown, and no stones mark the graves of the Farquharsons or their retainers, for Alisdair McDougal and Annie Ban are also buried there. The Black Colonel's broadsword and targe are preserved at Invercauld House, while the Colonel's cave in Glen Ey is visited by many every year.

The Cumins of Culter

On the north side of the North Deeside Road, about seven miles west from Aberdeen, stands Culter House, one of the most delightful old houses in the county. It is now the Boarding House of St. Margaret's School for Girls, Aberdeen, and despite the passing years, remains much the same as it was in the days of its builders, the Cumins of Culter.

Not very long ago, an unusual plant was found growing wild in the grounds of Culter House. It was not a plant of great beauty but its perfume was pleasant and rather like mignonette. At first its identity puzzled botanists, but eventually, it proved to be *Mitella diphylla* – 'Mitrewort' or 'Bishop's Cap' – a plant believed to be of American origin. How, or when, it was introduced to Culter House is a mystery although the most likely solution seems to be that it was brought from America by one of the Cumin lairds.

The Cumins – or Cummings as they were later called – came to Culter through the marriage of Philip, son of Jardine Cumin of Inverallochy, with Marjory, daughter and heiress of Sir Adam Wauchope of Culter in whose family the property had been since 1247. Although the Cumins rose to fame and fortune in Scotland, they were both vain and extravagant and indeed were always trying to 'show-off'. Hence they became known as the 'proud Cumins'. Tradition tells that at the marriage procession of Mary Queen of Scots to Lord Darnley, Cumin of Culter had his horse shod with silver shoes, so lightly nailed to the hoofs that, when he caused his mount to prance, the shoes fell off! As Cumin expected, the silver shoes were immediately picked up by the astonished people, truly amazed at the wealth and grandeur of the Cumin lairds of Culter.

Although a number of the Cumin family received the honour of knighthood, it was not until 1762 that Alexander Cumin, 14th laird of Culter, was created a Baronet of Nova Scotia by King Charles II. It was this laird and his wife Elizabeth Dennis of Puckle Church in Gloucestershire, who built Culter House.

Sir Alexander Cumin, 1st Baronet of Culter, and his wife Elizabeth, had a family of three – one son and two daughters – all of them born at Culter House. The son, also called Alexander, who eventually became 2nd Baronet of Culter and 15th laird, was born in 1690 and had a most astonishing career. As a young man, he held a commission in the Russian Army but returned to Scotland, studied

'They laid before His Majesty the grisly proof'

law and was called to the Bar. Sometime around 1725, Alexander married Amy, daughter of Lancelot Whitehall, a strange lady possessed of psychic powers, for as the result of a dream she had, the laird of Culter set out for America to visit the Cherokee Indians! With much difficulty, Sir Alexander made his way into the Red Indian country and at Nequassee attended a great gathering of Indians when he was elected Chief and Lawgiver of the Cherokee nation. Eventually, he returned to this country bringing with him seven Indian chiefs whose presence in London created quite a sensation. He presented the chiefs to King George II at Windsor Castle when they laid before His Majesty the grisly proof of their prowess in battle – the required number of scalps! Did any of the Cherokees visit Culter House? Probably not – but the American plant growing there – *Mitella diphylla* – may have been brought back from the Red Indian country by Culter's far-travelled laird.

A Good Name Gives Strength

There had been Hogs in Blairydryne for hundreds of years. The land on which they lived formed part of the Thanedom of Durris, in the Mearns, and the Hogs had been tenants there as long as people could remember.

Blairydryne lies on the northern slopes of the Grampians, that great mountain barrier which cuts off the north-east corner of Scotland from the rest of the country. The homestead of Blairydryne stood high on the west bank of the Sheeoch Burn, a swift-flowing stream which joins the River Dee at Kirkton of Durris. The ancient Cryne's Cross Pass over the Grampians passed through the lands of Blairydryne so that the homestead of the Hogs was a welcome sight to many travellers as they made their way down the rough, narrow between Craigbeg and Mongour to the valley of the Sheeoch and on to Kirkton. Blairydryne meant civilisation again after many miles of rough moorland.

Many famous travellers had crossed the Grampians by the Cryne's Cross Pass, and people in Glen Sheeoch often told the story of Edward I of England

– the 'Hammer of the Scots' – who, with his mighty army had journeyed that way and lodged at the old castle of Durris, the 'manor among the mountains', hard by the River Dee. But that was a long time ago in the year 1296.

Now it happened that, many years later, King James V – 'the poor man's king' – was travelling to Aberdeen to attend a Court of Justice. As was his custom, he travelled in disguise, pretending to be a wealthy farmer and calling himself 'the gudeman of Ballengeich'. It was late October in the year 1527, the end of a wet and stormy autumn, and the king was weary after a tiring journey over the Grampians. The route from Glenbervie had been hard – grim enough to chill the stoutest heart, for the hill streams were swollen and the track was everywhere littered with boulders carried down by the rushing torrents from the higher ground. There was a chill wind blowing from the north-east, and the mist, close and wetting, only lifted as the king and his friends reached Red Beard's Well at the head-waters of the Cowie.

As the mist cleared, the snug, thatched buildings of Blairydryne came into view and a welcome sight they were, backed by a sheltering belt of pines with the blue smoke rising from the chimneys. Naturally, the weary travellers guided their horses towards Blairydryne.

'A charter from King James V'

The barking of dogs brought Arthur Hog, tenant of Blairydyrne, from the steading. Down to the east he could see a party of five horsemen crossing the swollen Sheeoch Burn below the Mill. Slowly, they made their way up to Blairydryne, the youngest of the company riding forward to greet the farmer. He asked shelter for his master – the 'gudeman of Ballengeich' – and his companions, a request which was immediately granted, for Arthur Hog was a kind man and well-known for his hospitality.

The weather became worse. The ford over the River Dee at Mills of Drum was made impassable for the river had risen to a very high level. Consequently, King James and his friends were obliged to stay at Blairydryne for several days. Quite unaware that the 'gudeman of Ballengeich' was the king, Hog entertained his visitors generously and when the time came for them to leave Blairydryne, the 'gudeman' wished to make payment for the food and shelter they had received. Hog refused, explaining that, although he was not a wealthy farmer, he was proud to work on the land and proud of his good name. King James was very impressed and as they shook hands and parted, the king said 'always remember my friend, a good name gives strength'.

It was about a year after the king's visit to Blairydryne, that Arthur Hog received a mysterious package from none other than the Great Marischal of Scotland. It contained a charter from King James V – the 'gudeman of Ballengeich' – granting to Arthur Hog and his descendants the lands of Blairydryne in gratitude for the hospitable treatment he had received when travelling in these parts. Thus a kindly farmer became a laird and when in due course he recorded a coat of arms he selected for his motto *A good name gives strength*.

On the southern slopes of the Hill o' Fare, just over five miles from Blairydryne – as the crow flies – stands the delightful old Ha' Hoose of Raemore. It now forms part of the Raemore Hotel and many visitors admire the beautifully carved panel over its entrance doorway. Apart from its interest as a work of art, the panel is possibly the only surviving link in the story of Arthur Hog of Blairydryne and King James V for it displays the coat of arms of Arthur's descendant James Hog of Blairydryne – and the motto suggested by 'the poor man's king – *A good name gives strength*.

Brecbannoch of Monymusk

One of the most picturesque villages on Donside is Monymusk. Long before the time of recorded history, Monymusk had its civilisation, for relics of the Stone and Bronze Ages have been found in the district and, down the centuries, mention is made of Monymusk as being a place of some importance.

A little over six hundred years ago there came to Monymusk a tiny casket of great beauty and value. It is made of wood, bronze and silver, richly ornamented and studded with jewels, and is known as Brecbannoch. Brecbannoch is a Gaelic word, meaning, 'the speckled peaked one', for in shape Brecbannoch resembles a tiny house with a peaked roof and, being so richly ornamented, has a speckled appearance.

Brecbannoch came to Monymusk in a very curious way. The casket is first mentioned as being in the possession of St. Adamnan, who lived in the seventh century. He was one of St. Columba's missionaries, and founded the church of Forglen, in Banffshire, so that possession of the lands of Forglen and the custody of Brec-

16

bannoch went together, and could not be separated.

For long Brecbannoch remained at Forglen, and it was the solemn duty of the custodian of the casket to carry it before the Scottish army whenever it went into battle. Brecbannoch, you see, was of very special value, for it was credited with supernatural powers. Some say that it contained two bones of the great St. Columba himself, while others maintain that it was simply a treasured gift to Forglen from the Saint. At all events it was greatly valued by both Church and State.

In the year 1178 King William the Lion founded the Abbey of St. Thomas the Martyr at Arbroath. The Abbey commemorated the murdered Thomas à Becket and to it, from time to time, the king made various grants of land and treasures. So it was that, some time between the years 1204 and 1211, King William granted to the Abbey the custody of Brecbannoch, together, of course, with the lands of Forglen.

It was therefore the duty of the Abbot of Arbroath to carry Brecbannoch into battle, as the previous custodians had done. The little casket was carried round the Abbot's neck on a chain, and before a battle he blessed the soldiers and their arms, showed them Brecbannoch and prayed for victory. Even today certain churches continue this

'for many years the Abbots
of Arbroath carried Brecbannoch'

practice in war, but, of course, Brecbannoch is no longer used.

For many years the Abbots of Arbroath carried Brecbannoch before the Royal forces, and thus, in the year 1314, it was shown to the Scottish army before the famous Battle of Bannockburn.

The year after this battle, Bernard de Linton, Abbot of Arbroath, granted the custody of Brecbannoch and the lands of Forglen to Malcolm de Monymusk. He did so doubtless to avoid further military service, and so it fell to Malcolm and his descendants to carry Brecbannoch before the Scottish army in battle. This the Monymusk family did for three generations, but eventually Brecbannoch and the lands of Forglen passed to the Irvines of Drum, who in turn carried out the duties which fell to the custodians of the casket.

In some strange manner about which nobody knows, Brecbannoch returned to Monymusk, where it was kept in the Priory, an ancient religious house built towards the end of the twelfth century. In 1554 however, a great fire damaged the building, and many of its treasures were lost. Fortunately, Brecbannoch was saved from the flames and taken to the neighbouring House of Monymusk where it was preserved in one of the towers.

The House of Monymusk was then in the possession of the Forbes family, but in 1713 they sold it to the Grants. Brecbannoch remained at Monymusk from that date until 1933, when the laird, Sir Arthur Grant, Bt., decided to dispose of the casket.

Brecbannoch was therefore taken to London and shown at Christie's Saleroom. Its sale caused a great sensation among Scotsmen all over the world, and many travelled long distances to see it.

The little casket of St. Columba was purchased for the Scottish nation by subscriptions from friends of the National Museum of Antiquities of Scotland and by a donation from the National Art Collection Fund. It was thus saved for Scotland.

Should you ever visit Monymusk you will see the parish church, all that now remains of the old Priory buildings where Brecbannoch was kept and also, not far from the church, the tower of Monymusk House, where it rested for so many years. Of course, if you are very lucky and go to the Museum in Edinburgh you will see Brecbannoch itself.

The Warlock of Glen Dye

Between the village of Torphins and the bridge of Potarch is the hill of Craiglash. On the northern slopes of Craiglash is a great block of granite known as the warlock's stone, and it is here that, many years ago, the witches of the Torphins and Lumphanan district met for their frolics.

At Hallowe'en, a special frolic took place under the direction of a warlock, the name given to the male leader. The Craiglash warlock was Colin Massie, who is reputed to have attended the celebrations riding on a boar's back.

Colin stayed in a little cottage at Glen Dye. The household was made up of Colin and his old mother, a well-known witch, and a brother who was a dwarf. Colin was very tall, over six feet, with a deeply lined face and a large hooked nose.

Nobody would ever go near their cottage at night, for mysterious lights were often seen hovering over it and weird noises heard issuing from its closely shuttered windows. Even in daylight, people used to give it a wide berth in case the warlock or his brother should cast the 'evil eye' upon them. Many, in fact, used to carry a horse shoe with them if they were obliged to pass the Massies' cottage so that the 'evil eye' might be averted.

Witches and warlocks, you will remember, by the practising of Black Magic, could assume many shapes besides that of men or women, so Colin Massie's mother, whenever she went out on one of her trips, used to assume the form of a large white hare.

At this time there lived one, Ian Russell, the young laird of Tillyfumerie, a small property in the district. He was a fine-looking fellow and a keen hunter, few being able to out-ride or out-shoot him. Ian's mother was a daughter of the Douglas family of Tilquhillie. She was a proud and arrogant woman, very ambitious for her son, and determined that he would marry some great lady. Ian, however, was deeply in love with young Dora Harper, daughter of the laird of Ennochie, and intended to marry her, but whenever he mentioned this to his mother, she brushed the matter aside and refused to discuss it.

One evening when Ian was out on the moors with his gun, he sighted a large white hare. He thought it rather peculiar that there should be a white hare at that time of the year, for it was early autumn, but he took careful aim and fired. To his great surprise the hare ran off unhurt.

Ian was rather annoyed, for his marksmanship was the talk of the district, and he was seldom known to miss. Two days later he was coming home across the moors when he saw the same white hare in almost the same place. He took very careful aim and fired, but once again the hare bounded off unhurt.

He was now certain that this was no ordinary hare, but a witch in disguise. The next day he again went out with his gun carefully loaded, but in addition to shot he placed a small piece of silver down the barrel. He did this knowing that witches and warlocks can be killed by silver.

Ian roamed over the hills all day, but there was no sign of the hare. On the way home, however, the path led him past the warlock's cottage, and just off it he caught sight of the white hare. Trembling with excitement, Ian took careful aim and fired. He rushed forward to where the hare had been, and to his utter amazement found the warlock's old mother writhing in agony. He had shot the witch.

The sound of the shot brought the warlock and the dwarf to the door of their cottage, and when they saw what had happened to their mother, they rushed forward screaming fearful curses on the terrified young laird. The old witch died almost immediately, and Ian, shaking from head to foot, rode off home.

'the sound of the shot brought
the warlock and the dwarf to the door'

For three nights terrible sounds were heard to come from the warlock's cottage, and for several weeks neither the warlock nor his brother, the dwarf, were seen. Some said, in fact, that they had left the district, but nobody was brave enough to go and find out.

Some months later a great hunt was arranged, and many of the lairds from the district attended. The chase was long and hard, but ended abruptly for the quarry, a particularly fine stag, leapt over a gully and was dashed to death on the rocks below.

In the forefront of the hunt was Ian Russell, but his horse, unable to stop at the edge of the gully, shied and threw Ian out of the saddle, thus saving him from certain death, for the unfortunate beast lost its balance and plunged headlong into the gully. Ian was very fond of his horse, and climbed down to see if it could be saved. Imagine his horror and rage when he found, near the mangled body of his favourite steed, the warlock of Glen Dye sitting on a rock grinning at him with devilish glee.

Ian accused him of bewitching his horse, and drew his sword in order to run the warlock through, but Colin Massie merely raised his slender staff to meet the blow. When Ian's sword struck the warlock's staff, the blade buckled up, and Ian fell to the ground in a dead faint.

By this time the others in the hunt had arrived at the top of the gully. They had witnessed the scene between their friend and the warlock, but were powerless to help him, nor indeed were they anxious to do so, for everyone feared the supernatural powers used by the Massies.

To their astonishment Ian's friends saw the warlock lift the unconscious body and carry it off to his cottage. They followed at a safe distance and after they had seen the warlock enter and close the door they planned that one of their number should go forward in an endeavour to retrieve the body of the young laird of Tillyfumerie.

They drew lots and it fell to Murdoch Farquharson of Tillygarmont to go and ask for the body of their friend for they were sure that by this time the warlock must have killed him. Murdoch approached the cottage, sword in hand, and knocked loudly. He threw open the door and saw, before a roaring fire, the body of Ian Russell lying on the floor with the warlock bending over it while the dwarf was preparing some magic brew on the fire.

Murdoch immediately attacked the warlock but when his sword came in contact with the magic staff it did as Ian's had done and buckled up. Unable to do any more Murdoch fled from the cottage in terror, the warlock's terrible laugh ringing in his ears.

A full account of what had taken place was given to Ian Russell's mother who bade her servants to go to the warlock's cottage for the body of her son. They hesitated and despite her threats flatly refused to go to the place. Finally she had to go herself, stand before the cottage door and demand her son's body. Colin Massie, the warlock, only laughed at her and when she said that the wrath of the Douglases would fall upon the warlock if he did not hand over her son's body, he closed the door in her face. The proud woman had therefore to go home.

The terrible story came to the ears of Dora Harper. She knew that the Douglases did not approve of her friendship with Ian Russell but with great courage went that night alone to the warlock's cottage. It was a bright moonlight night and she timidly knocked at the door. It opened slowly and the horrible figures of the warlock and the dwarf appeared. The sight was too much for her and she swooned.

When she came round she found herself in the cottage beside the body of her lover. The dwarf was sitting by the fire and the warlock was watching her intently. Dora pleaded with the warlock to allow Ian's body to be taken home, and the earnestness of her pleadings, together with her beauty, softened the warlock's heart, and he consented. With his staff he touched Ian, who immediately sat up. His eyes fell on Dora and the warlock, who explained that his life had been spared because of his loved one's pleadings. Dora and Ian then left the cottage and walked to Ennochie in the beautiful moonlight.

Soon after this they were married, but from that time nothing more was seen or heard of the warlock of Glen Dye and his brother. The roof of their cottage fell, the walls crumbled and finally became overgrown with grass and heather. Nothing of it remains today, but a huge ash tree marks the spot where love triumphed over pride and force of arms.

St. Nathalan of Tullich

On the south side of the North Deeside Road before the entrance to the Pass of Ballater stands the ruined church of St. Nathalan.

St. Nathalan was one of St. Columba's band of missionaries who brought Christianity to Scotland, and it was he who settled in the Tullich district. This was in the seventh century.

St. Nathalan, or St. Nachalan as he is sometimes called, is reputed to have belonged to Tullich, and came of a noble family. He was a very talented man, and spent most of his time helping the poor people of the district.

He was most active in showing them how to till the soil, and such spare time as he had he spent in cultivating ground for himself. It was well that he did so, for one year there was a great famine in the district, and the people went to St. Nathalan for food. In his goodness he opened his stores of corn and gave to the starving people. They took so liberally of his grain, however, that when the sowing time came round again he found that he had no seed left.

Nothing daunted, St. Nathalan told his helpers

29

'he bound his right arm to his leg'

to take sand from the Dee and sow it on the fields in the usual way. When they had done this, St. Nathalan knelt down and blessed the place where the sand had been strewn. Everyone watched the fields very carefully, and sure enough a great crop was produced.

When autumn time came St. Nathalan's helpers gathered to assist with the harvest, which was the heaviest since he had come back to Tullich. Just as they were about to start cutting the grain a great storm arose, which laid the crop. The helpers were greatly dismayed, and cursed God for bringing this misfortune upon them. In a moment of anger St. Nathalan condemned God for His action, but soon the storm abated and the harvest was safely gathered in.

St. Nathalan was very sorry that he had given way to anger, and as a penance for his sin he bound his right arm to his leg, padlocking it securely and throwing the key into the River Dee. As he did so he vowed that he would not unfasten the lock until he visited the shrines of St. Peter and St. Paul in Rome.

After a long and trying journey, St. Nathalan reached Rome and visited the shrines of the Saints where he asked forgiveness for his sin. On his way through the streets of Rome he met a boy selling fish. He bought one and took it home for his evening meal. Imagine St. Nathalan's surprise when he cut open the fish and found the key to his padlock in its stomach. Greatly rejoiced he gave thanks to God for His forgiveness.

Having heard of this amazing incident the Pope sent for St. Nathalan and listened to his stories of the people of Deeside. He urged St. Nathalan to stay in Rome for a time and pressed him to become a bishop.

In due course, however, St. Nathalan returned to Tullich where, at his own expense, he built a beautiful church. He also built a church at Bethelny, now called Old Meldrum, and when he died at a ripe old age he was buried at one or other of his churches, but no record exists as to which one can claim the grave of this great and good man.

If you look at a map of the Tullich district you will read on it such Gaelic names as *Poll na h-iuchrach* (Key Pool) on the River Dee, *Sliabh Bheannachaidh* (Moor of Blessing), and *Dail Mallachaidh* (Haugh of Cursing), all of which commemorate the story of St. Nathalan.

The Laird's Man

A short distance from the village of Newburgh stands the lonely ruin of Knockhall Castle, at one time a stronghold of the Udny family.

If you had gone there about two hundred years ago you might have seen an unusual-looking figure wandering about the castle. This strange person was Jamie Fleeman, known locally as 'the laird o' Udny's feel'.

Jamie was born in the early seventeen hundreds at Ludquharn, in the parish of Longside, where the site of the Fleeman's cottage is still pointed out. Nearby the bridge of Ludquharn is Fleeman's Pot, a deep pool where Jamie's mother was drowned, so that early in life Jamie had to fend for himself. Though he had a sister Martha and a brother who was killed on board H.M.S. *Serapis*, Jamie is seldom mentioned in conjunction with them, being more often associated with the Udny family.

His early life was spent at the House of Ludquharn, where his quaintness was noted by the laird and his lady, for he was not like other boys. Jamie had a big round head, covered with dingy brown hair, always standing on end, while he generally wore a short doublet of sack-cloth. He never wore a hat and seldom wore shoes.

Jamie was a simple soul, but although he was known as 'the laird o' Udny's feel', he had a ready wit, was deeply religious, and very loyal to those who were kind to him. As he grew to manhood he left Ludquharn with a recommendation from the laird, and was taken into the household of the Udny family at Udny Castle, their principal seat in Aberdeenshire. There he stayed during most of his life, undertaking many important tasks for the laird.

Jamie Fleeman was fond of animals, especially dogs, and wherever he went he made friends with dogs. On one occasion he was sent from Udny to Edinburgh with an important letter for the laird who was staying there. Jamie made his way to the capital, but either he had not been told the laird's address or he had forgotten it, so that when he arrived at Edinburgh he had not the least idea where to find his master.

On such occasions Jamie was full of resource. He was seen walking along the streets of Edinburgh, not looking at the shops or people as you would expect a visitor to do, but staring intently at every dog he met. Suddenly he pounced on a dog and took it up in his arms. He entered a neighbouring shop and without a word to the surprised shopkeeper broke a length of cord from a hank lying on the counter and walked out again.

Jamie tied the cord round the dog's neck and with the words 'awa' hame wi' ye' set the dog down and followed it home. Sure enough he found the laird of Udny's lodgings for he had recognised his dog.

It was, in a way, through his love for dogs that Jamie Fleeman was able to save the Charter Chest of the Udnys at Knockhall Castle. Late one night, after the household had gone to bed, Jamie was sitting in his little room high up in the tower boring a chanter, for he played a little on the bag-pipes. As he sat at his task one of the dogs came up to his room and pawed him. Jamie, who was very intent on his work, spoke roughly to the dog, telling it to be off. A little later, however, it returned, and catching hold of Jamie, pulled vigorously at his doublet. 'What ails ye?' asked Jamie, laying down his chanter and following the dog to the stairhead. Imagine his horror when he discovered that the castle was on fire. He rushed to awaken the household and then, without thought for his own safety, dashed to the Charter Room, burst open the oaken door, picked up the Charter Chest, which normally took three men to lift, and hurled it through the window. For this action Jamie received a peck of meal and sixpence a week for life from the grateful laird.

'this strange person was Jamie Fleeman'

Jamie was well known in Aberdeen and at the various county houses which he visited. The Hays of Errol, the Guthries of Ludquharn, and, of course, the Udny's of Udny all had a place for Jamie in their kitchens. There is an amusing story told of his ready wit when one day a very grand person, thinking to raise a laugh at Jamie's expense, asked him 'Aren't you Jamie Fleeman, the laird of Udny's feel?' 'Aye,' said Jamie, 'Fas feel are 'e?'

Jamie died at his sister's house at Kinmundy in the early summer of 1778. He was buried at Longside, and if you ever visit the kirkyard there you will see the grave of this strange but fascinating character. At the ruinous castle of Knockhall the Charter Room can still be seen with the stonework of the window broken by the impact of the Charter Chest.

The Phantom of the Loch

On a beautiful site on the north bank of the River Dee, not far from the village of Banchory, stands the ancient castle of Crathes. It is the ancestral home of the Burnetts of Leys, and is one of the most beautiful castles in Kincardineshire.

Crathes Castle was built towards the end of the sixteenth century, but prior to this the Burnetts stayed at their stronghold on the Loch of Leys, a short distance north-west of the present castle. The Loch of Leys has long since been drained, but even today the site of the Burnetts' island home can still be seen.

In this stronghold lived Alexander Burnett, 8th laird of Leys. He married late in life, Agnes Lechtoun, a proud and ambitious woman who bore him a son also called Alexander.

When the boy was about six years of age the laird died, so that the duties of the Barony fell to Lady Agnes. These duties suited her well, for she was a domineering woman who loved to exercise her power over others.

One evening when Lady Agnes and the young laird, who was now nearly seventeen years of age, were sitting in the great hall of the castle a servant came running in to tell them that a nobleman and his retinue were calling for boats to bring them to the island. Lady Agnes and the young laird hastened to prepare for the arrival of the stranger, and in a short time Sir Roger de Bernard, from France, and his daughter Bertha were announced.

The de Bernards were related to the Burnetts through a cadet branch of the family which had settled abroad many generations before. Roger de Bernard had always longed to visit the ancestral home of the family, and as France was in a very unsettled state, he had taken the opportunity of bringing his daughter with him.

Lady Agnes and the young laird welcomed their relatives, and to celebrate the occasion a great banquet was arranged for the following evening.

The banquet was attended by many of the neighbouring lairds and their wives, and was a great success. After the feasting was over, Lady Agnes made a speech of welcome, which was replied to by Sir Roger. He thanked Lady Agnes and the young laird for their welcome, and said that he proposed to leave his daughter Bertha in the safe keeping of his kinsman while he returned to France to settle up his affairs, after which he would come back to Leys.

Alexander, the young laird, jumped to his feet and said that he was honoured to be allowed to look after Bertha de Bernard, and his words were applauded by all. But one of the company did not relish the arrangement. This was Lady Agnes, for she had already noted the friendship that had sprung up between her son and Bertha.

Lady Agnes had made other plans. She had decided that the laird of Leys should marry into the noble family of the Lords of Lorne, and she did not intend to let anyone upset her scheme.

In a day or two Sir Roger de Bernard bade farewell to his daughter, and left for France.

It was summer and Alexander, the young laird, and Bertha de Bernard spent most of their time in the saddle galloping over the hills and moors, and visiting friends and neighbours. Wherever they went they were popular, for their natural charm was a joy to see, and it was evident that they were deeply in love. Only the Lady Agnes disapproved.

In autumn, Alexander was obliged to go south to see the Abbot of Arbroath about a land dispute. He was uncertain how long his business would take him, and Bertha dreaded his going. She knew only too well that Lady Agnes resented her friendship with her son, so after he left Bertha hardly ever came down from her room in the tower.

Winter came and there was no sign of Alexander returning to Leys. Bertha fell ill of some wasting disease, and by the time spring came round little hope was held out for her recovery.

One day towards the end of June, Alexander returned home, but to his surprise there was no welcome awaiting him. Everything was quiet on the island. Something must be amiss. He crossed to the island and hurried to the great hall to find out what was wrong. Imagine his horror when, in the centre of the lofty room, he saw a bier on which lay his beloved Bertha.

His mother, Lady Agnes, crossed the room to comfort him. His brain reeled, and he felt faint. Alexander reached for a cup of wine standing on a table nearby, but his mother snatched it from his grasp and dashed it out of the window into the loch. Not a word was spoken between them, but Alexander understood. Bertha de Bernard had been poisoned.

It was a bitter blow for the young laird, but with the passage of time the memory of Bertha passed from his mind, and life at the castle gradually returned to normal.

About a year after Bertha's death, the family were sitting at supper in the hall. Suddenly the door swung open and into the room strode Sir Roger de Bernard. He had come back for his daughter.

On his way over from France he had heard of her death and, as he stood at the end of the table, he accused Lady Agnes of killing her. A terrible scene followed, and Sir Roger called down curses upon Lady Agnes who, he said, had broken faith with him and cruelly killed his daughter to further her own ends.

A curious chill seemed to enter the room. The hangings on the walls moved as if by some sudden wind. Lady Agnes sat bolt upright in her chair. She seemed transfixed with horror. Slowly she rose to her feet and screamed 'she comes, she comes!' – then with a horrible laugh sank to the floor dead.

When the awful memory of the tragedy was forgotten, Alexander Burnett, 9th laird of Leys, married Janet Hamilton, kinswoman to Archbishop Hamilton, and they were very happy together. Alexander decided that the old island castle of Leys would be better left to its tragic memories, so in 1533 commenced to build the present Crathes Castle, but did not live to see it completed.

Once a year, it is said, at the witching hour of midnight, the ghostly figure of a woman rises from the site of the old castle of Leys and glides slowly over the hill of Banchory to Crathes Castle. Some say it is the wraith of Bertha de Bernard going to

'the ghostly figure of a woman arises
from the site of the old castle'

43

see the beautiful castle built by her lover, while others maintain that it is the shade of Lady Agnes forever earthbound on account of her terrible crime.

Donald Oig of Monaltrie

About nine miles west from Ballater there stood, in bygone days, a house known as Monaltrie. Today there is still a house of that name, near the village, but it was built long after the time of the one mentioned in this story.

At the old house of Monaltrie there lived Donald Farquharson, or Donald Oig as he was called. He was a fine soldier and a very clever swordsman, who had distinguished himself at the skirmish known as the 'Trot of Turriff'.

It had been quiet for some time at Monaltrie – no battles nor quarrels with the neighbouring lairds – so Donald Oig set out for London. This was in the year 1640.

He reached London to find that great excitement had been caused by the arrival of an Italian who claimed to be the best swordsman in the world. Everyone from the king downwards disliked the Italian, for he was very overbearing and went through the streets with a retinue preceded by a drummer who issued his master's challenge. Everyone was frightened to take up the Italian's challenge, for he was reputed to be a wizard who could not be killed.

One day when the king and his courtiers were discussing the Italian swordsman the name of Donald Farquharson of Monaltrie was mentioned. The king enquired about him and was told that he was a gallant young Scot who had just arrived in London, and who had the reputation of being a very fine swordsman. The king sent for Donald, who made haste to obey the royal command.

On his way to the palace, Donald encountered the Italian surrounded by his retinue and heard the drummer issue his master's challenge. Donald immediately drew his sword and ran both drum and drummer through, crying as he did so 'hae deen wi' yer din'. The Italian was very annoyed because a crowd had gathered and were wildly applauding Donald for his prompt action. He challenged Donald himself, and arrangements were made for the duel to take place the following day.

The king was delighted when he heard that Donald had already accepted the Italian's challenge, and promised a reward if he managed to kill him.

That night Donald searched through all the taverns in London until he found the Italian's serving-man from whom he learned that his master bore a charmed life. Donald was rather dismayed when he heard this, but pressed the serving-man for more information. From him Donald learned that if the Italian's body was pierced by a sword and the sword withdrawn the wound would close immediately and the Italian would remain unharmed. This was the secret of his charmed life.

Early next morning a great crowd assembled to witness the duel between the Italian swordsman and Donald Oig. The duel was fast and furious, but Donald managed to pierce the Italian's body with his sword. 'Withdraw thy sword' cried the Italian, knowing of course that if Donald did so he would immediately recover and fight on. But Donald, remembering what the serving-man had told him, let loose the hold on his sword, left it in the Italian's body and exclaimed 'Lat the spit gang wi' the roast'. The Italian fell to the ground and died.

There was great rejoicing in London, and the king sent the reward – a bag of gold – to Donald, but when the crowd saw the gold they cried 'see the Scottish beggar pocketing our English gold'. Donald was very angry, and, taking the gold, he threw it to the crowd saying, as they scrambled to pick it up. 'see the English dogs gathering up the gold they could not earn for themselves, but a Scot won for them'.

Donald stayed in London for a time, where he became known as Young Donald of Albion, but soon city life began to bore him, and he longed for the hills of Deeside, so he returned to Monaltrie.

'he was a fine soldier and a
very fine swordsman'

He was ever ready for a fight, but in 1644 was killed in Aberdeen by a band of Covenanting soldiers who laid a trap for him.

Great was the sorrow of the people of Aberdeen, for Donald Oig was a favourite with everyone. He was buried in Drum's Aisle in the Church of St. Nicholas, Aberdeen, where many distinguished people of bygone days lie at rest.

The Trumpeter of Fyvie Castle

Within the broad lands of Fyvie there is no more picturesque spot than the old Mill of Tiftie. The mill is now ruinous and overgrown by vegetation, but the swiftly flowing burn still dashes its way through the tiny ravine above which the old mill stands.

At the Mill of Tiftie, nearly three hundred years ago, lived William Smith and his wife, Helen Black. William Smith was never called by his Christian name or surname but was, as is the custom in Aberdeenshire, known by the name of his holding. Hence William Smith, the miller of Fyvie, was known simply as 'Tiftie'.

'Tiftie' and his wife lived with their family a little way from the mill at a pretty house further up the burn. They were well-to-do country folk, and very anxious to see their family get on in the world.

Once a year the laird of Fyvie was wont to make a tour of all the properties on his estate, and so it was that, one morning in late autumn, the laird's great coach drew up at Mill of Tiftie. As was the custom on such an occasion, 'Tiftie' presented his wife and family to the laird, who was a kindly man and took a deep interest in the welfare of his people.

'Tiftie's' youngest daughter, Agnes, was the last to be presented to the laird and, as she was a very pretty girl, the laird had always a special word for her. Her brother and sisters did not like her to receive any special notice or to receive attention, but on this occasion the laird patted her on the head and gave her a kiss, saying, as he did so, that she was the most beautiful lady in all the lands of Fyvie.

Agnes, or Annie as she was generally called, was about seventeen years of age at this time, and very attractive. It is little wonder that, as she looked up at the laird's great coach with its costly trappings and coats of arms, she blushed when her eyes met those of the laird's trumpeter staring fixedly at her from his seat at the back of the coach.

The trumpeter was a handsome fellow from the Fyvie district. He was the son of a farmer called John Lamb, and had entered the service of the laird when quite young. Andrew, for that was his name, looked very handsome with his silver trumpet and fine livery, so it was little wonder that Annie and he became attracted to each other.

Their friendship grew, and every night Annie would steal out of the house and run to meet her

'they would meet on a little bridge'

lover who, of course, stayed at Fyvie Castle. They would meet on a little bridge that spanned the burn between the castle and the Mill of Tiftie, and talk for hours about their plans for the future.

One evening they were seen by Annie's brother, who told his father. He, being ambitious for his daughter's future, called Annie to his room and forbade her to see Andrew Lamb again. The girl refused – a terrible scene followed, and Annie was severely beaten.

From that day Annie's life was a misery to her. She had never been happy at home, for her brother and sisters were jealous of her and the affectionate place she held in the hearts of the neighbours. The laird too, on more than one occasion, said that she was a fine girl and that, had she been of noble birth, he might have wooed her himself.

Every day Annie was beaten and ill-treated at home, but she always contrived to meet Andrew in the evenings, when he did what he could to comfort her. Then suddenly a terrible thing happened to their love. The laird was called to Edinburgh, where he would be obliged to stay for a prolonged period. As Andrew had to accompany his master, Annie would be left alone to face the fury of her family.

On the little bridge over the burn where they had met so often they said their last farewell,

Andrew going with the laird to the capital and Annie back to the misery of her home.

For weeks she pined for her lover, growing paler every day. She became thin and weak, and because she could no longer do her share of the household duties she was beaten more frequently. One day in a great fury her brother struck her so brutally that she fell and broke her back.

For weeks she lay in great pain, always crying for her Andrew. On the 19th day of January, 1673, Annie Smith breathed her last, and was laid to rest in the churchyard of Fyvie. Her grave can still be seen with its simple inscription – Annie Smith, 'Tiftie's Annie', while high up on Fyvie Castle is a sculptured figure of Andrew Lamb, trumpeter of Fyvie, blowing his trumpet in the direction of the old Mill of Tiftie.

The Lady of the Tower

In a secluded part of Aberdeenshire, not far from the village of Tarves, stands the ancient tower-house of Schivas. It is a mysterious looking building, and was built nearly four hundred years ago by a family called Gray.

Long, long ago there lived within the tower-house one, Andrew Gray, Baron of the Barony of Schivas. He was a devout Roman Catholic, as were all the Grays, and he was a very determined man. His greatest pleasure was in enforcing his will upon other people. Andrew Gray had two children – George, who eventually succeeded his father as Baron of the Barony, and Mary, for whose future her father had made definite plans.

Although her father was a stern man, Mary enjoyed herself at Schivas mostly in the company of her brother, for they were very attached to each other. She grew up to be beautiful and clever, and was a true daughter of the Church of Rome. In records of her time there are many proofs of her fidelity to her faith, and it can be said with truth that she lived up to the family motto – *faith a holy anchor.*

When Mary was about eighteen years old she fell in love with her second cousin, John Leslie, a fine-looking youth of her own age. They were very happy together, and everyone looked forward to the day when they would be married, for they were beloved of all. There was one, however, who did not wish the marriage; this was Mary's father, Andrew Gray.

He did not think that John Leslie was good enough for the daughter of the Baron of Schivas, and had selected for his future son-in-law the heir of a noble Catholic Lord. On this marriage his mind was set, and despite the pleadings of his daughter and his son the marriage was arranged.

As the day of her departure from Schivas came nearer and nearer the more depressed Mary became. She did not like the nobleman that her father had selected to be her husband – he was old and thin, and reputed to be very greedy. Besides, she was very much in love with the gallant John Leslie.

Before Mary left home she planted a tree to commemorate her happy youth at Schivas, saying as she did so that with her happiness the tree would flourish. Many of the tenantry who were present shed tears as they heard these words, for Mary was a great favourite with them.

In due course Mary Gray arrived at the castle of her future husband, only to find that he had been called away to do battle in one of the many feuds of the time. It was with a sinking heart that she crossed the threshold of her new home, where it was obvious to her from the moment of arrival that she was to be little better than a prisoner. She was watched night and day, and when she went out, which was seldom, she was strongly guarded, for her future husband feared she might escape.

At Schivas, Mary Gray's tree wilted. The tenantry did what they could to make it grow but to no avail, and it looked as though it was about to die. There was great sorrow throughout the Barony.

Mary Gray, despite her guards, had always contrived to keep in touch with her lover, John Leslie, and one night, with his help, she escaped. All through the night they rode, and early next morning were married at a tiny wayside chapel.

Almost a year had elapsed since Mary had left the tower-house of Schivas, so when she arrived at her old home as the wife of John Leslie she found that her father had died some months before, and that her brother George was Baron of the Barony. There were great rejoicings at Schivas over her return and feastings which lasted several days.

But what of the tree? Needless to say it flourished from the moment of Mary's escape, and today is one of the grandest trees in all the lands of Schivas. You will see it if you ever go there.

'she planted a tree to commemorate
her happy youth'

58

In the upper part of the tower-house of Schivas is a tiny room known as Mary Gray's, and it is said that on the anniversary of her home-coming the happy figure of Mary Gray can be seen approaching the house, crossing the courtyard and ascending the narrow spiral stair to her little room. But nobody is ever afraid of meeting Mary's ghost, for she is obviously very happy and of course very beautiful.

The Knight of Wedderhill

On the south bank of the River Dee about six miles from Aberdeen is the parish of Maryculter.

Within the parish, about seven hundred years ago, was born Godfrey Wedderburn. His father, who had held high office in the household of the Pope, had retired to Maryculter, where he farmed the small property known as Wedderhill.

Not far from the Wedderburn's house, on a lovely bend of the Dee, stood the Preceptory of the Knights Templar. The Templar's Lands had been gifted to them by William the Lion in 1187, and there they built their Preceptory with its beautiful chapel.

The Knights were frequent visitors to the Wedderburn homestead, and their tales of hazardous adventure and thrilling experiences in the Holy Land made such an impression on young Godfrey that he decided to become a member of the Order whenever he was of age to join.

So it was that Godfrey Wedderburn became a Knight Templar, and in due course set out for the Crusades in the Holy Land, where he quickly distinguished himself by his many acts of bravery.

Unfortunately, however, Godfrey's courage and ever increasing desire for distinction on the field of battle were to prove his undoing, for one day, thinking to perform a crowning act of heroism, he attacked, single-handed, a fierce horde of opposing Saracens, and fell with many wounds. His companions, seeing him un-horsed and struck down by the ferocious Saracens, left him for dead and mourned the loss of their gallant friend.

But Godfrey was not dead although very seriously wounded, and when he regained consciousness he found himself being tended by a beautiful Saracen lady. The Saracen lady was very kind to him, and ere long she had nursed him back to health, and he was able to make for home.

Before Godfrey left the Holy Land she presented him with a charm of rare beauty, consisting of a plain gold circlet in which was set a gem of great brilliance. The charm she told him was proof against the dangers of war and disease, but could only be worn by those of spotless purity and unsullied honour. Godfrey thanked her for the charm and for nursing him back to health, and set out for home where he was received with great rejoicings by the knights who had thought him dead.

One Sunday morning, many years after Godfrey had returned from the Holy Land, as the knights were passing into the chapel for early Mass, their atiention was attracted by the figure of a closely veiled woman standing near the door, who eagerly scanned the features of every passer-by. When Godfrey approached she tore the veil from her face, and with a cry rushed forward, put her arms around his neck and kissed him. She was the Saracen lady who had saved his life in the Holy Land.

Godfrey was ordered to report to the Grand Master at the close of the service, and although he gave a full and truthful account of his friendship with the Saracen lady, his story was not believed by the Grand Master. The Master persisted in assuming that Godfrey had not acted with the honour that became a Knight of the Order, and in a fit of rage Godfrey sprang at him and struck him to the ground.

So great an insult was this considered that it was punishable only by death, but in consideration of his notable career, Godfrey was spared the indignity of dying by another's hand by being permitted to plunge the dagger into his own heart.

As he fell to the ground a piercing scream resounded in the woods and valleys, and the Saracen lady appeared. She snatched the charm from the dead knight's neck and dared the Grand Master to put it on to prove whether or not an injustice had been done. Contemptuously the Grand Master placed the charm around his neck – there was a blinding flash from heaven; a blue bolt of fire struck deep down into the earth where the Grand Master stood and he was seen no more.

When the Saracen lady saw what had happened she shouted for joy, and, snatching the blood-stained dagger from Godfrey's body, buried it deep in her own breast.

The Templars fled in consternation, refusing to return to the spot until daylight, when they found the bodies of Godfrey and the Saracen lady lying side by side – but there was no trace of the Grand Master.

Nearby the knights found the charm by means of which the stain had been wiped from two pure young lives and the swift and terrible vengeance of heaven brought upon the perpetrator of injustice. Fearing to keep the charm the knights cast it out into the fields where, it is said, on the anniversary of the terrible tragedy, it shines with a pale blue light.

Godfrey was not buried within the chapel precincts as was the custom for members of the Order, but in accordance with his dying wish he was laid to rest in a quiet corner near the Corbie Linn. The Saracen lady was buried nearby.

Not many years ago men used to tell with bated breath of having seen, at the midnight hour, a fully

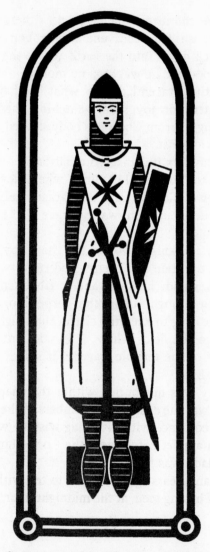

'he was received with great rejoicings'

armed Knight Templar galloping along the valley and over the hill of Kincaussie while near the Corbie Linn the shadowy figure of a dark-complexioned lady is said to glide through the neighbouring woods.

If you ever visit the parish of Maryculter you will see a deep depression in the ground, known as the 'Thunder Hole', which is said to be the exact spot where the Grand Master met his fate, and also the ruins of the chapel where the knights worshipped.

King William's Palace

In a lovely Aberdeenshire garden, not many miles from town, is a fine old gateway leading from one part of the garden to another. Over the entrance is a grey, moss-covered stone on which can be seen a Latin inscription cut on its face. The inscription reads – 'FUNDAVIT GULIELM R. SCOT. 1181' – which means 'Founded by William, King of Scots, in the year 1181'. Surely the inscription cannot mean that this beautiful garden – certainly a very old one – was founded by William the Lion, who reigned from 1165 to 1214? No! The inscription on the stone refers to some other place, a Royal Palace no less, and here is the story.

In the year 1181 King William the Lion decided to build himself a Palace in Aberdeen. As site for his new home he chose the south side of the Green – now a grey, dull and depressing place not at all suited for a Royal Palace: in King William's day it was a beautiful green open space covered with lush grass and surrounded by fine trees under whose shade, on warm summer evenings, the good people of Aberdeen were wont to sit and watch the great ships from distant lands riding at anchor in the estuary of the Denburn hardby the village of Fittie.

Here at his Palace in the Green, King William stayed whenever he happened to be in the north-eastern part of his kingdom which, to the great regret of the citizens of Aberdeen, was not very often, for affairs of state kept him mostly in the south. Perhaps it may have been because he could not stay in his palace as often as he would have liked that King William made a gift of it to a Religious Order in which he was greatly interested, the Order of the Holy Trinity then recently founded by Pope Innocent III.

For nearly 350 years the Trinity Friars – or Red Friars as they were called, on account of their red cloaks – remained in possession of the Royal Palace in the Green carrying out their daily tasks of tilling the soil, helping the poor of the town, writing and illuminating their beautiful manuscripts, and performing the many other duties that fell to them. Then came the Reformation. Many of their buildings were demolished and their treasured possessions plundered and destroyed by the angry mob. Most of the Red Friars fled to safety, and what buildings escaped damage remained empty for several years. In 1631, however, the derelict property of their Order was bought by an Aberdeen minister, thus King William's Palace

67

'they were wont to sit and watch the
great ships'

68

entered yet another phase of its interesting history.

The minister who bought the old Palace was William Guild, a man of great ability who later became Principal of King's College, Old Aberdeen. He was the son of Matthew Guild, a wealthy armourer, who had amassed a very considerable fortune on account of the ready sale for arms during the troublesome times of the sixteenth century. Matthew Guild took a prominent part in the affairs of his native town and, of course, was a member of the Hammermen Craft, and, through his father's interest in the Crafts, William Guild gifted to them the Trinity Friars' property.

This transfer to the Crafts was made in the year 1633, and shortly thereafter the Aberdeen Crafts established themselves in their new headquarters in the Green. They renamed Trinity Hall, to commemorate its occupation by the Red Friars.

The Aberdeen Crafts consisted of seven Trades – the Hammermen, the Baxters (Bakers), the Wrights and Coopers, the Tailors, the Shoemakers, the Weavers, and the Fleshers. They were of ancient origin, for it is known that in 1424 King James I passed an Act to encourage Craftsmen by allowing them to elect Deacons whose special duty it was to see that a high standard of workmanship was kept up in each Craft.

As in other towns, the Aberdeen Crafts played an important part in the life of the community. In the fifteenth century, for instance, certain of the Crafts were obliged to provide a number of fully armed men ready to defend the town should occasion arise. At the great Festival of the Halyblude they were prominent in the Processions and the Passion Plays which were acted on the Porthill, while one of their number was elected to direct the proceedings and given the title of Abbot of Bon-Accord.

For over two hundred years the Aberdeen Crafts remained at Trinity Hall in the Green but, when it was proposed to lay out the north railway line, it became obvious that in the interests of progress the ancient buildings must be demolished. In 1846, therefore, the buildings were pulled down and Trinity Hall in Union Street was built. It was vacated in 1964, a new Hall being built at the corner of Great Western Road and Holburn Street.

Should you ever visit Trinity Hall, or 'Tarnty Ha'' as it used to be called, you will see much that is of interest, for here you will see the beautifully carved Deacons' chairs with their coats of arms and quaint inscriptions, and the broad-swords captured by the Hammermen, Weavers, and Tailors who fought at the battle of Harlaw in 1411, when the Provost of the town, Sir Robert Davidson, was killed. You will also see the Charter Chests of the different Crafts, each with its three great locks so that they could only be opened in the presence of the three Craft Brethren holding keys.

The most treasured possession of the Crafts is, perhaps, the portrait of King William the Lion, reputed to have been given to the Trinity Friars by the king himself. By some miracle the picture escaped damage at the Reformation, and came into the possession of William Guild, who gifted it to the Crafts. Other fine portraits at Trinity Hall include Matthew Guild, the armourer, and, of course, one of William Guild, their greatest benefactor.

An interesting stone panel built into the wall tells of William Guild's gifts to the Crafts. It formed part of a very elaborate gateway to the Hall when it stood in the Green, with richly carved ornaments and coats of arms as well as a very ancient stone dating from the Trinity Friars' time, which had been incorporated in the gateway. This panel at Trinity Hall and the ancient stone are all that remain of the original building.

But where is this ancient stone now? Perhaps you may have guessed? Yes, it is the one in the beautiful Aberdeenshire garden with its puzzling Latin inscription –

'FUNDAVIT GULIELM R. SCOT. 1181'.

71

Sir James the Rose

Many years ago, there lived in the Parish of Crimond, a very gallant knight called Sir James the Rose. He had distinguished himself against the English on several occasions, for he was a brave man, practised in the art of warfare. Sir James was tall, broad-shouldered, and of powerful physique, a fine figure of a man as he rode at the head of his followers.

Sir James was very much in love with Matilda, daughter of the Thane of Buchan, who did not approve of his daughter's suitor, as he, himself, wished a marriage between her and Sir John the Graham.

Every evening Sir James and Matilda met to discuss their plans for the future, their trysting-place being a sauchen tree on the shores of the Loch of Strathbeg. There, they could talk without being seen or overheard, for it was a bleak spot, seldom frequented by the people of the neighbourhood.

Now, Sir John the Graham had a brother, Donald, a wicked and crafty man who was a real trouble-maker. Somehow, he had discovered the

'they met to discuss their plans for the future'

lovers' meeting place, and one night lay in wait
for them in an endeavour to discover their secrets.
By chance he was found by Sir James who challenged him to fight, and after a short encounter
the unfortunate Donald was mortally wounded.

Matilda, much perturbed by what had happened,
beseeched her lover to flee for his life while there
was still time. Her father and Sir John would seek
revenge immediately and, with their combined
forces, would doubtless annihilate Sir James and
his followers.

They met the following night at the Mill of
Haddo to bid each other good-bye, and Sir James
decided to take Matilda's advice. He told her that
he intended to make for the Isle of Skye, where
his brother lived, and there to collect a force strong
enough to beat his enemies. Matilda pointed out
that he could not do this for some time, and that
he would have to remain in hiding, for every inch
of the countryside was being watched, and most
certainly he would be caught. She would send a
messenger to Skye with a letter requesting Sir
James's brother to come to his aid. To this arrangement Sir James agreed, and the messenger was
despatched while he remained at the mill.

The messenger had not proceeded very far when
he was seized by some of Sir John the Graham's
men who threatened him with death if he did not

tell from whence he came. The terrified man told everything, and ere long the Mill of Haddo was surrounded.

Eventually Sir James's hiding place was discovered, and four of Sir John's men set upon him. Sir James was a great swordsman, and a fierce struggle followed in which the four men were killed. As the last man fell, Sir John crept up behind Sir James and pierced his side. It was a cruel and cowardly stroke, but Sir James swung round, and with his last once of strength ran his assassin through, and they both fell together, dead.

Matilda was overcome with grief and, it is said that, when her lover was laid to rest where he fell, she took his blood-stained sword in her hands and fell upon its blade so that in death they might be united.

At a spot called Battle Fauld, nearby the Mill of Haddo, the grave of this gallant Knight is still pointed out, while the old Ballad entitled 'The Young Heir of Baleichan' commemorates the incident in verse.

The *Crooked Mary*

In the bleak and wind-swept kirk-yard of Slains is
a simple tombstone with a brief inscription:

To
the memory of
Philip Kennedy,
in Ward
who died the 19th Dec., 1798,
aged 38.

It is a typical Aberdeenshire headstone – plain
and unobtrusive, with nothing to distinguish it
from countless others, but with this difference –
there is an interesting story behind it!

From Peterhead to Slains the North Sea coast
is broken by rugged cliffs, abounding in hidden
creeks and concealed caves which, from earliest
times, were the haven of the Viking, the buccaneer,
and the smuggler. In the eighteenth century smuggling was at its height and many Buchan fishermen
made a good living by lending a helping hand when
there was a 'run' – the name given to a landing of
contraband goods.

The most noted lugger engaged in smuggling at

'the carts could be heard approaching'

77

this time was the *Crooked Mary*, which had three points of call on the Buchan coast – Slains, Cruden, and Peterhead. The usual procedure was for the *Crooked Mary* to cast anchor some distance from land and wait until nightfall when a signal would be given from one of the three points. The cargo would then be loaded into the dinghy, rowed to land, hidden in some well-concealed cave or removed by a 'land party' in carts to some pre-arranged destination.

It was the 18th December, 1798, and a 'run' was on.

The *Crooked Mary* was sighted off the Buchan coast late in the afternoon, and a message was sent round to warn the 'land party'. The usual signal that a 'run' was on was to lay a plaid over the peat-stack, for a verbal message was considered too dangerous by the smugglers. Just before midnight, therefore, the 'land party', six in number, had collected together, with two carts, their wheels well greased and padded as were the horses' hoofs, so that there would be the minimum of noise. They were headed by Philip Kennedy, and when they reached the little bay, just north of Slains Kirk, where the loading was to take place, he gave the signal with his lamp to the *Crooked Mary*.

Everything appeared to be going well, but one factor had been overlooked. This was the 'gauger' or excise officer. He was a man called Anderson, who, with his two assistants, carried on a bitter and relentless war against smugglers. Somehow he had learned that an attempt to run contraband goods was to take place that night, so the three of them lay in wait for the first load. They selected for their place of ambush the narrowest point on the path which led from the bay to the main road, a spot well suited for their purpose.

They had not long to wait, for soon the muffled rumble of the approaching carts could be heard. When the carts were almost opposite, the 'gaugers' fired their pistols, but in the darkness their shots went wide of the mark. The terrified horses bolted, and the smugglers, with the exception of Philip Kennedy, fled into the night.

Kennedy stood his ground and gave fight, but he was no match for the three armed 'gaugers' who severely wounded him with their swords, leaving him lying where he had fallen. In the cold grey light of dawn the wounded smuggler crawled painfully to the kirk-yard of Slains, where he was found by his friends lying in a pool of blood and beyond help.

'If the others had been as true as I, the goods would have got through, and I would not be bleeding to death' were the last words of Philip Kennedy, who was laid to rest there.

The Wicked Laird of Balquhain

On the west bank of the River Urie, almost directly opposite the battlefield of Harlaw, stands a lonely ruined tower. It is the castle of Balquhain, ancient home of the Leslies, now derelict and forgotten, but in times past, the very mention of its name struck terror in all who lived in the Garioch.

The family settled in Aberdeenshire in the twelfth century, when one, Bartolf, received a grant of the lands of Leslie, from which they took their name. The Leslies were a wild and lawless family, wielding great power and exercising their feudal rights relentlessly over their wide domains.

The most notorious member of the family was, perhaps, Sir Andrew Leslie, 3rd of Balquhain. Known throughout the Garioch as 'Red Andrew', he bowed to no authority and did exactly as he pleased, terrorising the countryside for miles around. 'Red Andrew' devoted his entire life to fighting his neighbours, the Forbeses, only interrupting this self-appointed task to take part in the Battle of Harlaw in 1411, when, it is said, he was accompanied by eleven of his sons, all of whom were killed. This brief diversion over, Leslie

'Balquhain's out!'

returned to his tower and continued with his life's work – extermination of the Forbeses.

Sir Andrew lived for rapine and bloodshed, and when the word went round the Garioch – 'Balquhain's out' – there was a hasty gathering in of stock, barring of doors and shuttering of windows. Wives and daughters had to be hidden too, for, although 'Red Andrew' was married to gentle Isobel Mortimer of Craigievar, he liked a pretty face, and no woman was safe from his clutches.

Now, it so happened that there were great rejoicings among the Forbeses for their chief's son, the Master of Forbes, had become betrothed to a lady of surpassing beauty and accomplishment, Margaret Forbes, daughter of Sir John Forbes of Inveravon. Margaret, who was always referred to as the 'Fair Maid of Strathavon', lived with her devoted father and brother.

As the news went round, Sir Andrew eventually heard about the betrothal. Here, thought he, is a double opportunity – to carry off a beautiful lady, and at the same time annoy his sworn enemies, the Forbeses.

Leslie summoned his retainers, and when darkness fell they galloped from the grim tower of Balquhain to Inveravon. The Forbeses had retired for the night and all was quiet. Quickly the Leslies surrounded the house and forced an entry, murdering the servants and overpowering Sir John and his son. Margaret Forbes, screaming in terror, was bundled into a sack, dragged out into the night, and carried off to Balquhain.

The Forbeses raised the alarm – the Master of Forbeses betrothed had been taken by Balquhain! The young laird of Drumminoir rode out to rescue his future bride, gathering the family on his way – Brux, Corse, Monymusk, and all the others. They swooped down on Balquhain, vengeance in their hearts, but the wicked laird had fled. He had gone to the wilds of Bennachie, taking Margaret Forbes with him. There he hid from his enemies amid the crags of the Mither Tap. The tower of Balquhain was sacked and burned, but the lives of Isobel Mortimer and her young son were spared.

Sir Andrew remained in hiding on Bennachie for some time, but his thirst for battle proved too strong, and he came down to seek out his enemies. Near the Mill of Braco he encountered the Forbeses. A fierce struggle took place, and the Leslies were completely overcome by superior forces. 'Red Andrew' fought for his life with terrific ferocity, but it was obvious that he must be killed. His wife, who had witnessed the terrible conflict, rushed to his side and pleaded for his life, but he fell, mortally wounded.

On a beautiful site between the Mill of Braco

and the farm Broadsea are the remains of a tiny chapel. It is said to have been built by the gentle and pious Isobel Mortimer of Craigievar on the spot where 'Red Andrew' fell, and was buried on the 22nd day of January, 1420. It was endowed with a priest to say mass for the soul of her husband, Andrew Leslie, the wicked laird of Balquhain.

King Malcolm and the Herd-Boy

Centuries ago, the castle of Kindrochit, in Braemar, was a place of great importance. It was actually a Royal residence, for the kings of Scotland frequently stayed there when on hunting trips.

In the time of Malcolm Canmore, the constable of Kindrochit kept, for the king's amusement, a huge wild boar called Tad-Losgann, which he had captured during a hunting trip in Glen Quoich. The constable was very proud of his achievement, and had caused a special pit to be made for the boar on the rocky bank of the Clunie. A den, partly natural and partly artificial, formed its sleeping quarters. Tad-Losgann was, in fact, one of the 'sights' of Kindrochit and, whenever King Malcolm came on a visit, he always went to see him.

Tad-Losgann was quite small when the constable had captured him, but, as time went on, he became larger and larger, for he consumed a very considerable quantity of food. This did not worry the constable who, being a feudal lord, could do exactly as he pleased, so he simply issued a decree saying that every family in the district must supply in turn a living cow to appease Tad-Losgann's appetite! So Tad-Losgann grew bigger and bigger as the years went by.

Now, it so happened that a poor widow named McLeod was due to supply the required cow for Tad-Losgann. Widow McLeod lived in a little cottage in Glen Slugan with her son, Sandy, a lad of about fifteen. Her husband, a noted bowman in the district, had been killed in a fight at Corriemulzie when Sandy was but a few months old, so widow McLeod had a hard struggle to make ends meet, for there was not much of a living to be had in the Glen.

The cow was one of widow McLeod's most treasured possessions. It had taken her several years to make sufficient to buy the cow, and now, after all her labours, it was to be taken from her to feed Tad-Losgann. It was more than she could bear, and in her misery she cried out that, had her husband been alive, he would have put an arrow through the fat boar's body and thus saved many head of cattle, the loss of which poor people could ill afford.

Widow McLeod did not know that her son was listening to what she said, but he, lying awake in bed that night, devised a plan whereby he might save the life of his mother's cow.

Sandy had inherited his father's gift of archery, and had ample opportunity for practice as, during the long summer days when he was herding, he could make his own bows and arrows and shoot at the wild life on the hillsides. His bowmanship was, indeed, the talk of the district, and people said that, whenever he was old enough, King Malcolm would no doubt take him into his service as one of his archers.

The next day Sandy set about putting his plan into operation. First he made three new arrows, well barbed and carefully feathered, and these being to his satisfaction went up Cairn Laith. There he shot a large capercailzie which he took home, carefully hiding it from his mother. That night he went to bed as usual, but could not sleep for excitement.

About an hour before dawn he got up, dressed, collected his bow and arrows, took the capercailzie from its hiding place and set off for the castle. He forded the Dee below Dalgowan, made his way to Auchendryne, and finally reached the point he had in mind, a rocky ledge on the west bank of the Clunie overlooking Tad-Losgann's pit.

High on the castle wall Sandy could see the sentry on guard, and trembled when he thought that if he were discovered an arrow would wing its way towards him and the alarm would be raised. He would have to be very careful. Sandy peered into the pit. It was empty. No doubt

'he took aim with his best arrow'

Tad-Losgann would be asleep in his den. Very carefully Sandy took the capercailzie by the legs, swung it round his head once or twice, and threw it over the water right into the pit.

Sandy waited. It seemed like hours until Tad-Losgann came out of his den, sniffed the air, and then bounded forward to the carcase of the capercailzie. This was exactly as Sandy had planned. Very carefully he took aim with his best arrow and fired. The arrow sped forward and in silence Tad-Losgann rolled over dead – the shaft through his heart!

Somehow Sandy got back to the cottage, into bed and, exhausted, fell asleep immediately.

Next morning there was much excitement in the Castletoun. The constable's wild boar, Tad-Losgann had been found dead in his pit with an arrow through his heart. It had happened in the hours of the morning and under the very nose of the sentry, who had been put in chains for his negligence. King Malcolm was expected to arrive the following day, and there seemed little prospect of the mysterious bowman being found before then. He might come again to the castle, and next time it might be the sentry's body that would be found, or even the constable's – worse still, it might be the king's!

Throughout the district, however, there was

much secret rejoicing at the death of Tad-Losgann, for it meant that no more cows would have to be supplied to satisfy his appetite. Many indeed hailed the unknown bowman as a deliverer, and hoped that he would not be discovered.

The constable of Kindrochit was a very determined man, and he meant to find out who had killed the boar. He commanded that the arrow be taken from Tad-Losgann's body and brought to him. With great care the constable examined the arrow – it was well barbed and feathered – yes, and feathered in a peculiar way! All he had to do was to find out who in the district feathered his arrows in this manner. Accordingly he sent his men to search every cottage for arrows similar to the one that had killed Tad-Losgann. By nightfall the searchers returned with two arrows of a pattern similar to the one that had killed the boar – with them they brought Sandy, who was put in chains and thrown into the dungeon.

Next day poor Sandy was dragged from the dungeon and taken to the hall before the constable, who was greatly surprised at the prisoner's youth. He heard Sandy's reason for killing Tad-Losgann, but showed little mercy, condemning him to death on the following morning on the gallows on Greag Choinnich.

But what of Widow McLeod? She was completely overcome with grief when Sandy was taken away, and blamed herself time and again for what she had done. It was she who should go to the gallows, not her son. What could she do? The unfortunate woman knew that any appeal to the constable would be in vain, for he was a hard man who had little sympathy for the poor, so her only hope was to appeal to King Malcolm himself. She had heard that the king was expected at Kindrochit the following day, so she set out up the Clunie towards the Cairnwell Pass, by which route the king would come. Through that night and all next morning she waited, chilled by the cold and the fear that she might not succeed in her mission. In the late afternoon she saw a cavalcade approaching – it was King Malcolm and his party. Widow McLeod rushed forward and flung herself at the king's feet and pleaded for her son's life. The king was touched with her sincerity, and said that he would enquire into the matter when he reached Kindrochit, bidding her follow him there.

They arrived just in time, for the guards were leading the poor boy out to his execution as the Royal party were about to cross the drawbridge. The king spoke to the constable, and Sandy and his mother were called before them. The king said that Sandy would have a chance to save his life.

His mother would be placed on the rocky ledge across the Clunie from which he had shot Tad-Losgann, while Sandy would remain on the drawbridge. A peat would be balanced on his mother's head, and if Sandy succeeded in piercing it with his arrow, he would be allowed to go free.

Poor Sandy trembled when he heard the king's decisions, but he was a stout-hearted lad and realised that it was his only chance. He must not fail. He asked for his own bow and the two arrows which had been taken from him, and these were brought.

Across the Clunie, his mother stood with a peat balanced on her head. She smiled over to her son, and so gave him confidence. Sandy took careful aim and fired. His arrow pierced the peat and knocked it from his mother's head. There was a shout of joy from all who witnessed the incident, and the king summoned Sandy before him. 'A splendid shot,' said the king, 'but why ask for two arrows? You know that if you had failed with one you would have been hanged.' 'If I had missed the peat with the first arrow and killed my mother,' was the reply, 'the second arrow would have killed you.' A gasp of horror went round the assembled people, but King Malcolm laughed heartily. 'Well said,' cried the king. 'You are a hardy one – so henceforth you will be Hardy by name, and when you are of age you may join my archers.'

So Sandy and his mother returned to their cottage in Glen Slugan and lived in peace. He was afterwards known by the name of Hardy, but did not join the king's archers, for he never drew a bow again.

The Spectre of the Tower

Where rolls old ocean's surging tide,
   The Wine Tower beetling stands,
Right o'er a cavern deep and wide –
   No work of mortal hands.
                                    – *Old Ballad*

The Wine Tower stands on a rocky promontory not far from the town of Fraserburgh. Dashed by the spray of the North Sea, it has weathered the ceaseless assaults of time and tide for hundreds of years with all the characteristic doggedness of the north-east. Gaunt and forbidding, the Wine Tower is a plain rectangular building, several storeys in height and vaulted on every floor – a typical Scottish tower-house of the period to which it belongs.

In this grim and isolated tower lived Isobel Fraser. She was the only child of Alexander Fraser, Baron of the Barony, who owned extensive property in the district. He was a difficult man, very proud and ambitious, and deeply conscious of his ancient lineage, for his family had played an important part in Scotland's history since the twelfth century. Everyone, including his daughter, had to bow to his will, and he dominated his tenants with all the despotism of the Middle Ages.

It was late in November and the old tower looked more forbidding than usual. The sky was overcast and heavy with snow, and it looked as if a great storm were brewing.

Alexander Fraser was in a bad temper. A messenger had arrived the night before bearing a letter calling him to Aberdeen on important business. He bade his daughter good-bye, climbed into his coach, and set out for the south. Isobel watched the coach disappear from view, and then, with a shiver, for it was a bitterly cold morning, hurried into the hall where a cheery log fire was burning. She felt strangely elated, for she was seldom allowed out of her father's sight, and his absence from home, even for the short period of two days which he expected to be away, meant something of a relief to her.

Isobel looked out of the window across the grey North Sea. Snow was beginning to fall and it made a desolate picture. She crossed to the fire and took up her embroidery, singing at her work, for she felt happier than she had done for many months.

The snowstorm continued all day, and when darkness fell showed no sign of clearing. Late in the evening the household were startled by a loud knocking at the door. Who could be abroad on such a night?

The visitor was a man whose horse had gone lame and who, in the darkness and the drifting snow, had lost his way. He craved lodging for the night. This was the message brought to Isobel as she sat in the hall that cold winter night.

Isobel gave instructions that the visitor be brought in and his horse attended to, and in a short time Mr. John Crawford was announced. Isobel got quite a surprise when she saw that the visitor was a young man of her own age, and a handsome man at that. She bade him warm himself at the fire, and called for supper to be brought. They talked far into the night, and it was obvious that they were much attracted to each other.

Next morning John Crawford took his departure, and proceeded on his way to visit his aunt who owned a small property not far off. He thanked Isobel for her hospitality and promised to see her again, but she pleaded with him not to think of such a thing for her father would never consent to their friendship.

But their interest in each other proved too strong and, as the months went by, they had many secret meetings among the rocks. Their friendship grew to love, and John Crawford was determined to ask for Isobel's hand in marriage. He had a

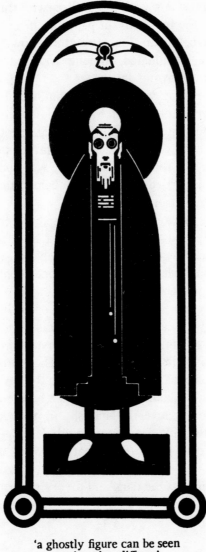

'a ghostly figure can be seen
pacing the cliff-top'

stormy interview with her father, who threatened him with the most direful penalties if he as much as saw Isobel again. John Crawford, however, was not to be intimidated, and he arranged to meet Isobel the following day.

Somehow their secret leaked out, and his loved one never came. Isobel had been locked in her room, and instead of finding her at the trysting-place he was confronted by her father's men. A brief struggle followed, but John was soon overcome and carried to the cave below the Wine Tower and put in chains.

That night a great storm arose. A fierce gale swept the coast and a huge sea was running. Mountainous waves dashed themselves against the rocks on which the old tower stood, defiant like its proud possessor.

By next morning the storm had spent itself and the sea was calm. Alexander Fraser called his daughter to him and requested her to accompany him for a walk along the cliffs. They set out together in silence, and he took her to the cave below the tower. It would be a great jest he thought for her to see her lover in chains, and doubtless in a more reasonable frame of mind. He, Alexander Fraser, would show them that his word must be obeyed.

They entered the dark and dreary cavern. In the

gloom he saw the dim outline of John Crawford lying on the green, slimy floor. He called to him to get up, but received no reply. Isobel ran forward and knelt by his side. His clothes were wringing wet, and he was stiff and white. She screamed in horror – John Crawford was dead – drowned by the incoming of the storm tide.

Isobel went back to the tower. Her father tried to comfort her, but she was beside herself with grief, and cried out that he had murdered John Crawford. A terrible scene followed, and Isobel rushed from the hall to the parapet-walk. She cried to her father that she would join her lover in death, and threw herself into the sea far below.

After the great tragedy, it is said, Alexander Fraser seldom left the Wine Tower, and on stormy nights, when the sea dashes against its rocky foundations, a ghostly figure can be seen pacing the cliff-top, stopping now and then as if listening to the wailing of the wheeling gulls.

The Witch of Findrack

On the first day of November falls the Feast of All Saints, or All-Hallows Day. The evening before it is called Hallowe'en.

Nowadays it is a happy time with parties and all the various games associated with Hallowe'en – apple-ducking, fortune-telling and many others, while the decorations used are peculiar to this time of year. There are black cats, owls, and bats, broomsticks and witches and, of course, the hollowed-out turnip with its terrifying face lit by candle-light and hung in some dark corner to frighten the unwary. It is all very jolly now, but it was not always so, for, four hundred years ago, Hallowe'en was the dreaded night when the witches and warlocks held their frolics.

Between the Bridge of Potarch and the village of Torphins is the Hill of Craiglash on the lower slopes of which is a great boulder of granite known as the 'Warlock's Stone'. Around this stone the witches of the district met on Hallowe'en.

There were many such places in Aberdeenshire where witches and warlocks gathered to practise Black Magic, but in the records that have come down to us it would appear that the Torphins coven was the most notorious. There was the customary twelve witches and the warlock in the coven, and the names of five of the witches are known. These were Helen Rogie who stayed at Findrack, Jonet Lucas from Pitmurchie, Margaret Clark who stayed near Lumphanan, Jonet Davidson from Sundayswells, and Margaret Ogg from Marywell. All these places are in the vicinity of Torphins, and the ruins of some of their cottages can still be seen.

Unless they were obliged, no one would ever have thought of going out on Hallowe'en in case a witch's path should be crossed and the 'Evil Eye' cast on them, for witches were credited with amazing powers. It was therefore accepted that when John Mackie, a farmer from Bogenchapel, encountered Helen Rogie, the witch of Findrack, trouble would be in store for him.

Helen Rogie lived alone in a tiny cottage on the lands of Findrack. It was little more than a hut built of rough stones, gathered from the land, while its roof was thatched with broom. Two tiny openings served as windows, so that inside the cottage 't was very dark, the peat-reek from the open hearth adding to the gloom. It was a desolate-looking place, visible for some distance as it stood on the western slopes of Learney Hill.

'he encountered Helen Rogie'

Nobody cared to pass Helen Rogie's cottage even in daytime through fear of being bewitched, for she was reputed to be a very wicked and revengeful woman. Her mother had been a witch before her and had taught her daughter all the secrets of Black Magic with which she was familiar. Helen's mother had been burned at the stake in Aberdeen for witchcraft, so her daughter's hatred for those neighbours whom she considered to have been instrumental in causing her mother's death was, in a way, understandable.

John Mackie was a well-to-do farmer in Bogenchapel, where he stayed with his wife and daughter. On this particular Hallowe'en it so happened that he had been across to Inchley to see about some stock, and was rather late in returning home. Just as he was turning into the road leading to his farm he encountered Helen Rogie on her way, no doubt, to the Craiglash Frolic.

It all happened so suddenly that John Mackie never exactly knew what took place. His dog, Paddy, had heard his master's footsteps on the road and come to meet him. Usually a quiet, friendly beast, Paddy suddenly took fright at the unexpected appearance of Helen Rogie and rushed at her, tearing her plaid and skirt. It was all that John Mackie could do to prevent the dog from biting the witch, but somehow he managed to get Paddy away and, when he turned round to see the extent of the damage, Helen Rogie had disappeared.

John Mackie then made his way home with Paddy, who had got a good thrashing for his behaviour. He recounted the incident to his wife who was quite upset when she heard the story, for she knew something of the spells cast on people by Helen Rogie.

Next morning, when John Mackie went out to the byre, he was greatly surprised to find his dog lying dead in the close. He remembered the encounter of the previous night and feared that Helen Rogie had been busy with her spells. The following week his wife fell and broke her leg, while within the year his daughter died.

All these things and many more were attributed to Helen Rogie and so, with several other witches from the district, she was brought before the Assizes for trial.

When the officers went to her cottage to arrest her they discovered that she had gone, and for many days they searched the surrounding country. At the first sign of danger, Helen Rogie had fled to Learney Hill where, in a tiny cave, she hid until discovered by the officers. In her cottage they found ample proof of her witchcraft – images in soft lead, pictures of the people she had bewitched, coloured threads, twisted wire, and many strange writings.

It was late one afternoon in the month of April, 1597, when a grim procession made its way across Aberdeen's Castlegate to the gallows on the Heading Hill. There, all was in readiness for carrying out the sentence of death on the witch. The materials had been collected for the burning – twenty loads of peats, a boll of coal, four barrels of tar, four fathoms of rope, and, of course, a stake.

The Assizes, under the Chancellorship of John Irvine of Pitmurchie, had ordered that she be strangled, burned, and her ashes scattered on the Hill. The sentence was carried out. The executioner received his fee of 13s. 4d. for his work and so ended the miserable life of the unfortunate Helen Rogie, witch of Findrack.

Osbarn, the Smith

On the southern slopes of Ben Newe, at a little place called Greenstyle, there lived, nearly six hundred and fifty years ago, a family called Osbarn. There were three sons in the family and, as was the custom at that time, each was known by the occupation which he followed. Thus the eldest was known as Osbarn, the Smith, for he plied the trade of blacksmith in the district.

The Osbarn family were rather unpopular in the neighbourhood, especially the Smith, but, being a good craftsman, he was always kept busy, for there was much work to be done in those far-off days.

Not many miles from his home stood the great castle of Kildrummy, then at the very height of its fame as one of Scotland's most formidable strongholds. There was generally a large garrison at the castle, fully armed and horsed, so it was not surprising that Osbarn, the Smith, obtained the position of blacksmith to the castle. At Kildrummy there was plenty for him to do, for, besides shoeing horses there were arms to repair, stout hinges and bolts to make, massive iron 'yetts' to be constructed, and farm implements to be made. Many, indeed, envied Osbarn, the Smith, for he was well paid for his services, and lived in comfort and security within the great fortalice.

But Osbarn was not happy. He had one unfortunate weakness – greed. To him, money was the only thing that mattered in the world, and he went to all extremes to increase his wealth. He therefore had no loyalties and no friends.

It was the summer of the year 1306. King Robert the Bruce had been defeated at Methven, near Perth, and had taken to the hills. Eventually he made for Aberdeen, where the queen, his daughter Marjorie, and his brother Nigel, met him. Others joined the Royal party, but the approach of the English drove them to the west, and at Dalry, in Argyll, the king was obliged to withdraw before the superior forces of his bitter enemy, John of Lorne. As the Royal ladies could no longer endure the hardships of a campaign, the king sent them to Kildrummy Castle under the escort of his brother, Nigel, and the Earl of Athol.

There was great rejoicing at Kildrummy when the Royal party arrived. In the party were the queen, the Princess Marjorie, the king's sister Marie, and his brother Nigel, the Countess of Buchan, and the Earl of Athol, together with many other knights and ladies of rank. But their rejoicing was short lived. Word reached the castle that Edward of Carnarvon, Prince of Wales, son of the terrible Edward I, was making for the north.

In haste, the queen, with Princess Marjorie and the other ladies, fled to the sanctuary of St. Duthac's Chapel at Tain, while Nigel Bruce remained at Kildrummy to meet the assault of the English. The castle was prepared for siege. Vast stores of food and munitions of war were collected and stored in the great hall, the wall-heads were manned, the massive studded doors of the gatehouse were barred and bolted, the iron 'yetts' swung in place and padlocked, and the drawbridge raised. All was in readiness for the attack.

On 1st August, Edward of Carnarvon crossed the Mounth and, with glittering arms and fluttering pennants, encamped at Kildrummy. The siege of Kildrummy Castle has gone down in Scottish history as one of the outstanding events of the fourteenth century, and the dogged resistance of the Scots under Nigel Bruce ranks as one of the most courageous acts of the War of Independence. Many and furious were the attacks made by the English, but without success, for the Scots were determined to hold out for their king. The days dragged on to weeks, and there was no sign of the defence crumbling.

But what of Osbarn, the Smith? During the

preparations for the siege he had been very busy, for there was much to be done. To withstand an onslaught such as the English would deliver, the iron-work of the castle had to be inspected and tested so that it was only when the opposing army was encamped without the walls that Osbarn had some respite from his labours. It was then that he began to think about his future prospects.

Should the castle fall to the English the whole garrison would doubtless be put to the sword, so he had little hope of survival and none of adding to his wealth, whereas, if the garrison succeeded in holding out, he would be in the same position as before. But could they hold out? Not indefinitely. Then he must think out some way in which he could make provision for the future and increase his wealth.

The weeks passed and the outcome of the battle had not been decided. Osbarn, the Smith, became very restive, and his greedy brain was ever at work devising schemes whereby he might make money from the desperate position in which he now found himself. At last his mind was made up. He would go to the English camp and betray the castle.

At dead of night, therefore, he crept from the shadows of the dark, defiant stronghold, and made his way to the English camp. He was taken by the guards to the prince's tent, where he explained

'they poured the molten metal down his throat'

who he was and how he hoped to help the English to capture the castle. There was a long consultation among the leaders, and they prepared a plan in which Osbarn would play an important part. This they did for they were uncertain whether Osbarn intended to betray them in turn to the Scots, thus the part allotted to the blacksmith was not without much risk. He had to return to the castle and, on a signal being given from the English camp, set the building on fire.

His part in the plan was not exactly to Osbarn's liking for, should he have been missed from the castle he would have difficulty in explaining his absence. He had not bargained on returning. Osbarn weighed the question very carefully; what would he receive if the plan succeeded? The prince told him that he would have as much gold as he could carry. The blacksmith could hardly believe his ears – as much gold as he could carry! He was a very strong man, and could carry great weights – why, he would be the wealthiest man in all the broad lands of Mar! It was well worth the risk.

It was still dark when he returned to the castle, and he went straight to his forge. As he had no friends in the garrison he had not been missed, so he set about planning how best he could set fire to the castle. His forge was situated close to the great hall, a wooden building with a thatched roof.

It would be a simple matter for him to throw a piece of red-hot metal on the roof, for the forge door faced the hall. The thatch would readily catch fire and spread to the timbers. This would be his plan when the signal came.

To the blacksmith the next few days seemed interminable in their length. The siege went on as before. Then suddenly the signal came. Osbarn was hammering out a coulter for a plough-share at the time, so he put it into the fire again until it was red-hot. He plucked it from the glowing embers and threw it high on to the roof of the hall. It glowed like a tiny star among the thatch, which burst into flames, spreading to the timbers, so that ere long the whole building was a blazing mass. The heat was terrific, and many of the garrison had to seek protection on the wall-heads. The fire spread rapidly to the other buildings within the courtyard and complete confusion reigned in the castle. At this point the English pressed home an attack. The massive oaken doors caught fire, the 'yetts' twisted in the heat, and it appeared that the castle must fall.

In the night, however, Nigel Bruce and his men built up the openings caused by the fire, and in the morning the siege was continued, but not without increased difficulties for the poor Scots, for all their food and ammunition had been destroyed in the fire. It was only a matter of time before Kildrummy Castle would fall. Hunger, not the English army, forced the defenders to give in, and early in September the castle surrendered to Edward of Carnarvon.

Nigel Bruce was taken prisoner and hanged at Berwick and the garrison put to the sword. But not Osbarn, the Smith.

Osbarn presented himself at the English camp and claimed his reward for betraying the castle – as much gold as he could carry. This was the greatest moment of his miserable life. The English seized the unfortunate man, bound him hand and foot, melted a quantity of gold and poured the molten metal down his throat – as much as he could carry! A grim end to his life of greed and treachery.

St. Monire of Crathie

It had been a long journey for an old man, and the weather had not been good, for, although it was the month of May, there was still much snow on the hills. In many places the track had been completely washed away where some raging mountain stream, swollen by the melting snow, had carried everything before it in its rushing torrent. This made travelling both difficult and tiring.

The old man was St. Monire. He had rested for a day or two at the Hospice of Glenshee before attempting the last part of his journey, which would bring him to Deeside.

St. Monire was a Celtic missionary who had felt the call to go among the wild peoples of western Aberdeenshire and, although now well on in years, his undaunted spirit, fired with the new faith, urged him on. No amount of dissuading on the part of his fellow-missionaries had been of the slightest use, for his mind was made up to go into the Highlands and open up a new way of life for the peoples there. So he took his departure from the mission station in the south and headed north for the valley of the Dee which was known to be a strong outpost of paganism.

It was late afternoon when the saint arrived within sight of the hamlet of Auchendryne. Tired and hungry, he rested on the slopes of Morrone before entering the village. He ate heartily of the bannocks which the good people of the Hospice had insisted on his taking, and he quenched his thirst at a nearby spring. Thus, much refreshed, he set out for Auchendryne, wondering, as he approached the crude huts that comprised the hamlet, what sort of welcome he would receive.

St. Monire had scarcely reached the outskirts of Auchendryne when the inhabitants, headed by their pagan priest, approached him demanding to know whence he came and what he wanted. The saint explained that he had come from the south to teach them about God and to bring peace and love into their homes. He was bringing to them a new religion called Christianity, which would enable them to live a fuller and richer life than they had ever known before.

The pagan priest, who was obviously very hostile, replied that they did not wish to hear about the new religion. He urged the assembled people to attack the saint by telling them that he was an evil spirit come to cast a spell over them and destroy the village. In terror the simple folk fell upon St. Monire, beating him with sticks and stoning him from Auchendryne.

It was indeed a miracle that St. Monire escaped with his life, and, with aching limbs and heavy heart, he made his way along the high bank of the Dee into the west.

By nightfall he had reached the clachan of Inverey, with its handful of huts that housed the people of this remote community. There he begged for food and a night's lodging, but a warning from the pagan priest had preceded him and he got but scant hospitality, for no one would let him rest the night in his hut. St. Monire was very weary, and felt that he had but a short time to live. Perhaps, he thought to himself, he had been wrong in not accepting the advice of his fellow-missionaries when they had tried to dissuade him from undertaking the difficult journey to the north. Still, he had obeyed the call within him and so might die, well content, knowing that he had done his best.

In the gathering darkness he crossed the gurgling waters of the Ey, wandered up the slopes of Creag a' Chait, and bore west to the lower slopes of Càrn na' Moine where, completely exhausted, he sank down among the heather.

The sun was high in the heavens when the saint awoke next morning. He was faint with hunger

and parched with thirst. Very stiffly he staggered
to his feet, stumbled a few steps and fell headlong
into the heather again. He lay very still. He felt
sure his end was approaching and he began to pray.
His prayer finished, St. Monire imagined he heard
the trickling of a stream nearby. Surely this could
not be. He sat up and looked round and there, but
a few paces off, was a beautiful spring bubbling
from the hill-side, crystal clear, and flowing from
a tiny crevice in the rock.

St. Monier dragged himself to the spring, asked
a blessing in the name of the Virgin Mary, then
drank deeply. With each draught of the refreshing
water new life seemed to course through his veins.
He stood up, and in great gratitude gave thanks to
God for his deliverance.

It was a lovely morning. A short distance up
Càrn na' Moine a herd of deer nibbled the fresh
green moss, the deep-throated call of grouse could
be heard from Glen Ey, while, above all, sounded
the distant rumble of the Connie Falls. St. Monire
rejoiced with nature as he stood there on the hill-
side – but there was something near him, a presence,
out of harmony with his feelings. He turned round,
and there before him stood the pagan priest who
had followed him from Auchendryne.

The priest looked at the bubbling spring and
declared that it would be cursed forever as it had

'he gave thanks to God for his deliverance'

quenched the thirst of an evil spirit. He gathered
a handful of mud and threw it in the eye of the
spring, calling upon his pagan gods to dry it up
forever. The water stopped flowing, and in great
exultation the priest cried that it had been cursed.
Very quietly St. Monire replied that the spring
could not be cursed for he had blessed it in the
name of the Virgin Mary, therefore it would bubble
up again and shine brightly like the faith he
brought.

To the priest's amazement the spring bubbled up
and flowed as before. He fell upon his knees before
St. Monire and asked forgiveness.

Thus the saint won his first convert on Deeside
and a very important one too, for, when they
arrived back in Auchendryne, St. Monire was
received as an honoured guest. For some time he
worked and taught among the people of Auchendryne, then set off east down the valley to Crathie.
There he spent most of his time and built a church,
the ruins of which can still be seen on a knoll between the Lebhal and Rhynabaich. Later, however,
St. Monire set off again on his travels in the hills
and founded another church at Balvenie, in
Banffshire.

St. Monire died in the year 824. On Deeside,
where he worked so hard, he is remembered by
the name given to a deep pool on the Dee not far

from Balmoral Castle – Polmanaire, while, within living memory, there used to be held at Crathie on the 18th of December every year a Fair called Feillmanaire – St. Monire's Fair.

His well on the slopes of Càrn na' Moine still gives forth an abundant stream of clear, refreshing water. For long it was called by the name of Tobar Mhoire – the Well of Mary – and was visited by many sick and suffering souls for, ever since it saved St. Monire's life, has been credited with miraculous powers.

Edom o' Gordon

Standing sentinel amid the wild, heather-clad hills of upper Donside is Corgarff Castle, the scene of that grim tragedy so vividly and beautifully described in the ballad 'Edom o' Gordon'.

The tragedy, it is true, was but one incident in the long and bitter struggles between two great Aberdeenshire families, the Gordons and the Forbeses, but among the many gruesome and terrible outrages committed during the troubled times of the sixteenth century, it stands out as being the most awful and horrible.

The castle of Corgarff was built as a hunting lodge for the Elphinstone family who, in 1507, were granted the Forest of Corgarff by James IV. In the year 1561, however, it was acquired by John Forbes of Towie who, with his family, settled down in the lonely glen, a bleak, almost uninhabited district, the sanctuary of deer and mountain birds.

It was the summer of 1571, and John Forbes of Towie had left his wife, Margaret, and their family at Corgarff Castle while he accompanied his kinsman, Lord Forbes on a foray against their sworn enemies the Gordons. All that summer,

Margaret Gordon, her sister the Lady Crawford, the young laird, Alexander, and the rest of the family enjoyed the beauties of the secluded glen – the wild hill-sides, the swiftly-flowing burns with their foaming cascades, the songs of the birds, and the gay flowers on the river bank. Autumn followed and cast her rich mantle over the glen. The hills took on a deep purple hue, the trees became a brilliant yellow, while the hips ripened to a lustrous vermilion. Never had the glen seemed so beautiful and peaceful.

October came and the higher hills had their first dusting of snow. It was cold and damp, and the glen presented a grim and forbidding appearance. A message had come to the castle telling of a fierce and bloody encounter between the rival families at Tillyangus, and that a party of Gordons under the notorious Adam Gordon was ravaging the Forbeses' territory.

The Gordons were a lawless family who had earned for themselves the name 'gey Gordons', not 'gay' as it is sometimes spelt today – a word with a very different meaning. Since the Battle of Corrichie in 1562, when the old Earl of Huntly had been killed and his third son beheaded at Aberdeen, the Gordons had been on the side of Mary, Queen of Scots. Alexander, the second son, had been taken prisoner and convicted of treason, but later reprieved by the queen, while Adam, the fourth son, had obtained pardon in consideration of his youth.

It was an unfortunate day for the Forbeses when, by the queen's clemency, Adam Gordon was pardoned, as he proved to be the most blood-thirsty of the family, his many acts of cruelty and barbarity making the name Edom (Adam) o' Gordon dreaded throughout the country. It was this Gordon who now harried the territories of the Forbeses.

Adam Gordon had two good reasons for thus ravaging the lands of the Forbeses. Firstly, there was the old family feud – an excellent excuse for any form of brutality – and secondly, there was the cause of the queen which legalised his actions, for the Forbeses were opposed to Mary.

When John Forbes of Towie left his wife and family at Corgarff Castle, he did so with every confidence, for, apart from any sudden sally by roving bands of caterans which the building was well able to withstand, he did not anticipate any large-scale attack, for the castle was situated at the head of the Don valley, and well out of the way of the conflicting families. As all the able-bodied men were soldiering, only the servants were left with his family. Such confidence, however, was Adam Gordon's opportunity.

Early one morning, as the grey mists were lifting

from the hills, the look-out in the cape-house of Corgarff observed a party of Gordons coming up the glen. The cry was raised 'The Gordons are coming!'

There was much activity in the castle. The courtyard gate was made fast, the wooden ladder giving access to the castle doorway pulled up, the great studded door bolted and barred, and the massive iron 'yett' swung in place and securely padlocked. The grim tower of Corgarff awaited attack.

A short distance from the castle the Gordons halted. Their leader, Captain Ker, and two others advanced under the flag of truce, and, when within hailing distance of the tower, called to the defenders that he came from Adam Gordon of Auchendoun, and demanded that they surrender in the name of Queen Mary.

There was a hurried consultation within the castle. Margaret Forbes who, in the absence of her husband, assumed command of Corgarff, asked for twelve hours respite to consider the proposal of surrender. This was granted, and Captain Ker and his two companions withdrew, rejoining their party.

It will never be known exactly what happened after this or why the Gordons should have broken faith. At all events they made a sudden rush at the castle, scaled the courtyard walls, piled brush-

'the terrified screams of the trapped
defenders could be heard'

wood, peats and logs and every available piece of inflammable material against the tower and set it alight. Soon the entire building was a blazing inferno. The heat was terrific, for the pine logs were resinous and the peats were dry. The terrified screams of the trapped defenders could be heard above the crackling of the burning timber. For them there was no escape. Every window in the tower, as was the practice in those days, was heavily barred on the outside by stout iron grilles. The entire houshould, twenty-seven in number, were doomed to perish.

In the cold light of the following dawn the charred and smouldering shell of Corgarff Castle presented a gruesome spectacle, and it was some time before anyone in the neighbourhood had courage enough to approach the blackened ruin, although the Gordons had marched away as soon as their foul work was done.

The bodies of the unfortunate victims were taken to the kirkyard at Nether Towie and buried amid the great lamentations of the whole country-side.

In those days, however, there was little time for sorrow, the one thought was for revenge. It was hardly a month later when John, the Master of Forbes, received word that Adam Gordon was in Aberdeen. With all speed he made for the town.

The two families met at the Crabstane, and a fierce and bloody battle ensued. Once more the Forbeses were defeated and obliged to retire.

Little remains to be told. The persecution of the Forbeses continued for some time until the sudden death of Adam Gordon at Perth in 1580. Many years later the castle of Corgarff was again in occupation by Government forces during the '45, but the Forbeses never returned, for they built another castle at Towie.

Corgarff has recently been restored but Towie is in ruins, while the Crabstane in the Hardgate at Aberdeen marks the site of the famous encounter.

The Maiden Stone

In the Chapel of Garioch district of Aberdeenshire, at the farm of Drumdurno, there lived, many years ago, a family called Maitland. They were honest, hard-working farm folk, much respected in the neighbourhood, where their ancestors had farmed for many generations.

The Drumdurno family numbered five – James Maitland and his wife, Mary, their two sons, John and George, and their daughter Janet. Janet was the youngest of the family and, although only seventeen years old, was capable of doing all the countless duties about a farm that are a woman's lot.

It was summer, and they were early astir, for the day was to be spent gathering in the peats which, earlier in the season, her father and brothers had cut and set up to dry. James and Mary Maitland, their two sons, and the 'orraman' were all going to help in the moss, while Janet stayed at home to look after the farm and prepare supper. Before setting off, the boys jokingly reminded her that the supper would have to be a special one, for they would be ravenously hungry when they returned in the evening.

Once the family were safely away to the moss, Janet prepared for her day's baking, for she knew what country appetites were, and she always liked to make something tasty for her brothers. By ten o'clock she was completely engrossed in her baking, and sang gaily as she worked at the deal table in the centre of the stone-flagged kitchen.

It was a perfect summer day, and Janet could not resist going to the back door to have a look up at the moss. In front of her the grotesque outline of the Mither Tap stood out in all its grandeur, the peat-moss reaching to its lower slopes. The birds were singing merrily while the drone of the bees made her drowsy. She thought of the family working up there on the moss and hoped that nothing would happen to any of them among the treacherous peat-hags.

The thought of how her grandfather had lost his life in the moss was always brought to mind at this time of year, for it had been in August, eight years earlier, that the accident had happened. Old James Maitland had gone over to the moss one evening to see if the peats were ready for bringing in. There was a thick haar over everything, and Mary Maitland had cautioned the old man before he set out to keep on the track. By nightfall he had not returned, so Janet's father with some of the neighbours had gone to look for him. In the darkness no trace of him could be found, but next morning his body was discovered in a deep, water-filled peat-hag. Doubtless he had strayed from the track in the mist and fallen into the quagmire from which he had been unable to get out.

Janet would always remember how her father had taken her and the boys into his room and told them never to go on the moss after dusk, and even in daytime to keep to the track. One day, he hoped, there would be a good cart road through the moss which would make the peat-carrying so much easier and certainly much less dangerous.

With these thoughts in her mind, Janet returned to the kitchen and her baking, and soon was hard at work again and singing merrily.

Suddenly there was a knock at the door, and a very pleasant voice called out 'May I come in?' Janet was quite taken by surprise, but managed to say, 'Why, of course.' The visitor came into the kitchen. He was a youth of about her own age, very handsome, with dark hair, sparkling eyes, and a ready smile. He walked over to the deece by the fire, sat down, and watched her baking. Soon they were talking and laughing together. Janet spread a bannock for him with butter and jam, which he ate heartily, praising her cooking and telling her that she was the most beautiful maid in all the Garioch.

'a great boulder took her place'

Janet laughed loudly when he asked her to marry him, and when she teasingly replied, 'Maybe,' he asked what he might do to win her hand. Thinking of the workers out on the moss, Janet said that to win her in marriage he would have to make a good road from the moss to the door of the house in time for bringing in the peats that night! She laughed boisterously when she thought of the impossibility of her bargain, but the youth said nothing, only bade her good-bye, and left as quietly as he had come.

Busy with her work about the house, Janet soon forgot her visitor but, thinking that it would soon be time for the family returning, she went to the door to see if there was any sign of them. She looked up towards the moss. Something appeared to be shining on its surface – what could it be? She had never noticed it before. Janet looked again, then the awful truth dawned upon her – it was a paved path! Her visitor had been a warlock in the guise of a handsome youth, and she had made a bargain with him!

She ran into the kitchen, sank down on the deece, and wept. What could she do? After a time she crept back to the door, and to her amazement the path was only a few feet from the threshold! Terror seized her, and she ran out into the close as the final slab was laid. The path to the moss was complete!

The warlock appeared, but not in the guise of the handsome youth. He stood before her in all his ugliness, and claimed her for his bride. Janet ran for her life, and the warlock gave chase. Suddenly she felt herself being caught by the shoulders. She screamed in terror, and fought with all her strength. The poor girl cried out that rather than marry a warlock she wished that she might be turned to stone. 'Your wish will be granted,' said the warlock, in great fury, and called on the evil spirits to help him. There was a blinding flash, the earth trembled, a column of smoke rose from the ground where Janet stood, and when it cleared away a great boulder had taken her place. She had been turned to stone, and since that fateful day the monolith has been called the 'Maiden Stone'.

Should you ever visit Chapel of Garioch, you will most likely be taken to see the 'Maiden Stone' standing not far from the farm of Drumdurno. You will be shown the peculiar carvings upon it – The Warlock, in the guise of a fierce-looking elephant, the evil spirits which helped him in his wicked practices, and the symbols of poor Janet, the 'Maiden' – her mirror and her comb.

Some people of course, have other ideas about the origin of the 'Maiden Stone', but the Garioch folk prefer to adhere to their own story!

The Mysterious Fire
at Frendraught

It was the beginning of the year 1630, and the lairds of Frendraught and Rothiemay were engaged in a bitter dispute over the common boundaries of their lands – the family feuds which for generations had over-run Aberdeenshire showed little signs of terminating.

Sir James Crichton of Frendraught belonged to a great and powerful family, as did the laird of Rothiemay, who was related to the Marquis of Huntly, so that the dispute, however trivial it may have been at the outset, soon became a matter of major importance. Accordingly, the Crichtons of Frendraught set out to exercise what they believed to be their lawful rights only to be met by the Gordons of Rothiemay, who fully intended to uphold the honour of their family.

Early one morning, therefore, the two families met at the mutual boundary of Frendraught and Rothiemay, and a sharp struggle between them followed, during which Gordon of Rothiemay was severely wounded. The Gordons retired to Rothiemay Castle with their wounded laird, who died soon after his arrival. The Rothiemays immediately demanded blood-money for the death of their laird, and the Marquis of Huntly, acting as the Feudal Superior of both families, fined Sir James Crichton the sum of 50,000 merks. The fine was paid, but with strong misgivings, for it was felt by the Crichtons that the Marquis, being related to the Rothiemays, had not acted in an unbiased manner.

Shortly after, another dispute arose, this time between Sir James and the laird of Pitcaple. Robert Crichton, a kinsman of Sir James, had shot young Pitcaple through the arm.

The Marquis of Huntly was again the feudal superior of both parties, so he summoned them to appear before him at Bog of Gight. Possibly in an endeavour to allay the rancour of the Crichtons, the Marquis decided in favour of Sir James, but the decision infuriated Leslie of Pitcaple to such an extent that he vowed he would avenge the insult to his family. At this the Marquis was rather perturbed, for he did not wish any more trouble. He decided, therefore, that Sir James must be escorted home to Frendraught in case the Leslies should waylay him.

Accordingly, he instructed his son, the Viscount Aboyne, and John Gordon, the new laird of Rothiemay, and several others to accompany Sir James home to Frendraught. The journey was accomplished without incident, and, on arrival, the party was welcomed by Lady Crichton, who invited them to say overnight. The invitation was accepted with hesitation.

Now the castle of Frendraught consisted of two separate buildings – an old tower and a later house linked together by a wooden gangway built at the first floor level. Sir James and his Lady, together with their servants, occupied the later house, so that the guests were accommodated in the old tower.

That evening there was a gay dinner party at Frendraught – Sir James and his Lady, the Viscount Aboyne, the Laird of Rothiemay, George Chalmers of Noth, Captain Rollock and others. They dined merrily, and everyone was in the best of spirits.

Just before midnight the guests retired, the Viscount to the vaulted room on the first floor, where he was attended by his servant, Robert Gordon and his page, English Will. On the floor above was John Gordon of Rothiemay and his servants, while on the third floor was Chalmers of Noth, Captain Rollock and their attendants. The party had wined and dined well, and were soon asleep.

In the small hours of the morning the Viscount was awakened by smoke entering his room. He got up and rushed to the door, to make the alarming discovery that the building was on fire. His first

'the Viscount was awakened by smoke entering his room'

thought was for his friends on the floors above. He raced up the spiral staircase which gave access to the upper rooms to arouse the sleepers. His brave action cost him his life for, just as he reached the upper floor, the wooden gangway linking the tower to the later building caught fire, thus cutting off all means of escape, for all the windows of the tower were heavily barred on the outside.

Before long the old tower of Frendraught was a blazing mass, and in the terrible conflagration every guest perished.

Next day the charred bodies were discovered and laid out in the stables at Frendraught, and news of the tragedy sent to the Marquis of Huntly. Sir James and his Lady were immediately suspect, and the Marquis applied to the Privy Council in Edinburgh to hold an investigation.

On the 13th of April, 1631, a Committee, specially appointed by the Privy Council, met at Frendraught to investigate the tragic fire. The evidence was carefully sifted, and it was found that the fire could not have been caused accidentally.

The Committee's finding only increased the suspicion against the Crichtons and, even after John Meldrum, a brother-in-law of Leslie of Pitcaple, had been condemned to death for implication in the incident, the Crichton family were still suspect.

Sir James lived very quietly after the terrible tragedy, and in 1651 became an elder of the Kirk of Forgue, making several gifts to the church. But Lady Crichton left Frendraught and went to stay with her daughter at Kinnairdie, where she lived in solitude, suspect to the end of her life. She was excommunicated by the Kirk in 1654.

The truth about the Frendraught fire will never be known, and it must remain one of Aberdeenshire's unsolved mysteries.

Bibliography

Annals of Aberdeen. W. Kennedy. 1818.

Buchan. J. B. Pratt. 1858.

Bennachie. J. Longmuir. 1869.

Deeside Tales. J. C. Michie. 1872.

Loch Kinnord. J. C. Michie. 1877.

History of the Aberdeen Incorporated Trades. E. Bain. 1887.

Annals of Lower Deeside. J. A. Henderson. 1892.

History of the Valley of the Dee. J. Mackintosh. 1895.

Church and Priory of Monymusk. W. Macpherson. 1893.

Family of Burnett of Leys. New Spalding Club. 1901.

Corgarff Castle. W. E. Smith. 1901.

Life of Jamie Fleeman. J. B. Pratt. 1912.

The Black Colonel. J. Milne. 1921.

Kildrummy Castle. W. D. Simpson. 1923.

Crathie and Braemar. J. Stirton. 1925.

Fyvie Castle. A. M. W. Stirling. 1928.

The Celtic Church in Scotland. W. D. Simpson. 1935.

A Buchan Tower house. F. Wyness. 1943.